The Home Book of
Viennese Cookery

THE HOME BOOK OF
Viennese Cookery

by
TRUDE JOHNSTON

FABER AND FABER LIMITED
3 Queen Square London

First published 1977
by Faber and Faber Limited
3 Queen Square London WC1
Printed in Great Britain by
Latimer Trend & Company Ltd Plymouth
All rights reserved

© *Trude Johnston 1977*

FOR KEMBALL, TIMMY,
GUY, CHRISTINE AND WILLIAM

British Library Cataloguing in Publication Data

Johnston, Trude
　Home book of Viennese cookery.
　1. Cookery, Austrian
　I. Title
　641.5′9436′13　　TX721

　ISBN 0–571–10923–3
　ISBN 0–571–11178–5　Pbk

Contents

Within each section the recipes are alphabetical and at the same time grouped by type, e.g. all the different chocolate cakes are grouped under 'chocolate' within Cakes and Gâteaux, and are also themselves grouped alphabetically.

Contents

Introduction

I was born in Vienna and lived there until Austria was occupied by the Germans in 1938. I came to England, where I met my future husband. We were married shortly before the war in 1939, and it was then that I realized that I could not cook at all. My husband was in the army and when my mother came from Vienna to stay with me, this was the obvious moment for me to learn to cook.

In those two months my mother taught me the basic principles of cookery—Viennese style. In the many years which have passed since then, I have added a lot of experience to that basic knowledge. I was helped from the start by the fact that I enjoyed experimenting with new dishes, and by the memory of the good fare on which I had been brought up in my Viennese home.

My husband and our four children, as well as our guests, seem to enjoy my cooking and this made me decide to try and pass on my experience to other cooks.

Although my recipes are 'Viennese', they come from all the other Austrian regions, as well as the far corners of the Austro-Hungarian Empire, for they have all become part of Viennese cookery. Vienna so dominates Austrian cookery that one finds country pubs and restaurants proudly advertising their cuisine as 'Wiener Küche'.

For most of my recipes I am indebted to my mother's handwritten collection, and to one left to her by our gardener's wife. This lady had been head cook in a big house before her marriage, and always came to help out in our kitchen for big dinner parties—her cooking as well as the variety of her recipes were second to none. I also collected recipes from friends and relations each time I visited Vienna after the war.

Although I try to reproduce the Viennese taste and appearance, there are important ways in which my own cooking differs from the methods I remember in our kitchen at home. I use every labour-saving device which is not an affront to good cooking. Oven-to-table heatproof dishes save a lot of washing-up of saucepans, and roasting meat in a pan with a lid, or wrapped in foil, saves a lot of oven cleaning. I cannot imagine being without my large pressure-cooker which cuts down cooking time drastically and preserves the taste of the food, nor without my electric mixer and blender. My mixer's motor is not strong enough to turn yeast dough and this is the only dough I knead by hand. I took eagerly to icing sugar, which I believe is not known in Vienna, but I still make boiled sugar icing in the Viennese way for all special occasions and in particular for Sacher Torte. You will not find a recipe for puff pastry, which I have not made since the excellent ready-made packets became available. I continue to make my shortbread pastry because I think it better than the bought variety, and because it is quick and easy to make. I buy all pasta ready-made, as well as dried beans, peas and continental lentils, and quick-dried peas and French beans. On the other hand, there is nowadays enough fresh fruit available all the year round to make a fruit salad which tastes better and costs less than any tinned variety. I use only homemade bread-crumbs. I save all dripping from roast pork, beef and poultry as well as making dripping from suitable left-over fat. I also save most vegetable stocks for use in soups and gravies. I do not, however, give a recipe for making sauerkraut; it is a long and wearisome process and not worth the effort when you can buy sauerkraut at a very reasonable price and of good quality.

For some—to me mysterious—reason most authors of cookery books seem to consider 'margarine' a dirty word. Yet I myself, and many other cooks I have discussed the subject with, use margarine in cooking more than we use butter. I have never yet eaten bread spread with margarine instead of butter, but it would not occur to me to use butter in a dish where the taste of the fat is entirely drowned by other strong tastes, such as onion. In baking I use

Introduction

margarine everywhere because it gives greater lightness in cakes which are to rise. I have discovered from experienced Viennese cooks that margarine was used there for baking even in the palmy days before 1939, for this very reason. However, any cook who so wishes can replace margarine by butter in my recipes for short-bread pastry and for most biscuits. And when butter and margarine are almost the same price, I use melted butter on all my steamed and boiled vegetables.

There are some tools that are particularly useful in Viennese cookery. To beat escalopes successfully you need a meat hammer. A slicer consisting of a sharp blade embedded in a wooden board slices vegetables to the required thickness quickly and efficiently. Cake tins with detachable bottoms make the turning out of even the most fragile or sticky cake easy. A metal upright grater is needed to carry out some of the instructions, as is a hand-turned grater for grating, rather than grinding, nuts, chocolate and so on.

All my original Viennese recipes are in grammes. There are 28·35 grammes to the ounce but—for simplicity's sake—I have converted them at the ratio of 30 g to 1 oz. This is a perfectly satisfactory ratio as the proportion of all ingredients is adjusted accordingly. When following the recipes, do not attempt to mix both metric and imperial measures.

In these days of high meat prices, I find myself using my Viennese recipes more and more. There are many savoury soufflés, and cheese, vegetable and egg dishes, which may take more time than, say, grilling a chop, but which are much cheaper as well as being nutritious, without being starchy, making the extra effort worth while. And many of the recipes use only the cheaper cuts of meat.

Over the years I have slightly adapted some of my recipes and 'invented' others, always in the Viennese style, which I am glad to include in this book before they are lost.

Table of Comparative Oven Temperatures

	Electricity		Gas
	Fahrenheit (F)	Celsius (C)	
Very slow	250–270°	120–140°	½–1
Slow	300–350°	150–180°	1–3
Moderate	350–375°	180–190°	3–5
Moderately hot	375–425°	190–220°	6–7
Hot	425–475°	220–240°	7
Very hot	475–500°	240–250°	8–9

Precise oven temperatures are not given in the recipes: the above table should be used as a guide.

Quantities

Most recipes in this book will serve 5 to 6 people: as a general guide, one can allow 5 to 6 ounces of meat per person and 6 to 8 ounces of fish. Some desserts, cakes and biscuits will provide 8 to 10 servings. It is very difficult to lay down exact quantities as these depend so much on varying appetites and on what other dishes are being served at the same meal.

Soups

Soups play an important part in Viennese cookery. In the traditional Viennese household soup is served at least once a day, usually for lunch. The best Viennese soups have beef or chicken stock as their basis. Of the two, white or brown beef bouillon stock is the most typically Viennese. It can be served with dozens of different garnishes, but I have confined my recipes to those which I regularly make myself and which are inexpensive and quick to produce.

WHITE BEEF BOUILLON STOCK   WEISSE RINDSUPPE

This is the basic soup that is then served with one of the garnishes that follow.

1 kg (2 lb) shin of beef, or braising beef, or brisket of beef, or oxtail	240 g (8 oz) each: carrots parsnip
240 g (8 oz) beef bones	celery
150 g (5 oz) melts	onion
150 g (5 oz) cheapest liver	3½ l (6 pints) salted water

Present-day beef prices are so high that I sometimes substitute melts for all the beef and at the same time double the amount of carrots and celery to improve the taste. Crush the bones with a meat hammer, chop the vegetables roughly and bring to the boil from cold in the salted water. Add the cut-up liver and melts and when the water boils add the beef in one piece. Cook slowly but steadily in a covered pan for 2 to 3 hours, until the beef is tender. Discard bones, melts and liver. The meat can be served surrounded by the neatly cut vegetables with a little stock poured over the top. Taste the stock and add salt and pepper if needed; a beef bouillon cube may be needed if no beef was used in preparing the stock. Let the stock get cold, skim off the fat and use as directed in the following recipes.

For BROWN BEEF BOUILLON STOCK, brown the meats and vegetables in 120 g (4 oz) fat before boiling with the crushed bones. The fat is, of course, skimmed off the cold stock.

BATTER DROPS

EINTROPF

Make a batter from:

    60 g (2 oz) plain flour   *1 egg*
    3 tablespoons milk   *salt*

The batter should be runny. Pour the batter through a funnel or from a jug into 1 l (2 pints) lightly boiling beef bouillon stock. Hold the funnel about a foot above the boiling soup and move it criss-cross over the soup. Serve as soon as possible.

FRIED BATTER DROPS

GEBACKENE ERBSEN

Make a thin batter as for plain batter drops. Heat fat or oil in a pan and let the batter drip into the hot fat through the back of a coarse metal grater. The Viennese name for this garnish is 'fried peas' which will give you a guide-line as to the size and shape of the batter drops. Let as much batter drip into the fat at one time as will lie in a single layer. Allow the drops to get golden brown and crisp before lifting them out with a fish slice, letting the surplus fat drip back. Keep warm and serve in a separate little dish to accompany 1 l (2 pints) beef bouillon stock.

EGGS

EIER

Let a whole egg slip into each bowl of very hot white beef bouillon stock. Serve at once.

LIVER 'RICE'   LEBERREIS

45 g (1½ oz) white bread, soaked
   in water and squeezed well
90 g (3 oz) liver
a little finely chopped onion
sprig of parsley, chopped

30 g (1 oz) fat
1 egg
salt, pepper, marjoram
homemade soft breadcrumbs as
   needed

Scrape the liver with a blunt knife and then put it with the soaked bread through a sieve or mix in an electric blender. Soften the onion and parsley in the fat and stir into the purée, together with the egg, salt, pepper and marjoram. If the mixture is very runny, add breadcrumbs to give some body. Press through the back of a coarse metal grater into 1 l (2 pints) lightly boiling beef bouillon stock. Bring the soup back to the boil and simmer for a minute. Serve as soon as possible.

CHEESE 'RICE'   KÄSEREIS

30 g (1 oz) butter or margarine
1 egg
45 g (1½ oz) grated cheese

15 g (½ oz) homemade
   breadcrumbs
salt
1 l (2 pints) beef bouillon stock

Cream the butter with the egg, stir in the cheese, breadcrumbs and salt. Press through the back of a coarse grater into the lightly boiling stock, bring back to the boil and simmer for 1 to 2 minutes. Serve at once.

PANCAKE NOODLES   FRIDATTENNUDELN

60 g (2 oz) plain flour
1 egg
1 dl (4 oz) milk

pinch of salt
fat for frying the pancakes

Make pancakes with a batter made from the flour, egg, milk and salt. Roll up each pancake and cut it across into noodles about 3 mm (⅛ in) wide. Serve in a separate dish to accompany 1 l (2 pints) beef stock.

SPONGE CUBES
SCHÖBERLN

2 eggs' weight of flour   pinch of salt
2 eggs, separated

Fold the flour, egg yolks and salt into the stiffly beaten whites of egg. Spread on a greased and floured cake tin and bake in a moderately hot oven for about 15 minutes, until the sponge has browned a little and has shrunk from the sides of the tin. Turn out on to a wooden surface, cut into 1 cm (½ in) cubes and serve in a separate little dish to accompany 1 l (2 pints) hot bouillon.

CHEESE SLICES
KÄSERÖSTSCHNITTEN

60 g (2 oz) margarine   salt, paprika, grated nutmeg
120 g (4 oz) grated Parmesan or   1 French loaf, cut into 1 cm
    other grated cheese   (½ in) slices
1 egg

Cream the margarine with the egg, stir in grated cheese, salt, paprika and grated nutmeg. Spread the mixture on the lightly toasted bread slices, and return to the grill for a moment, until the slices are hot and crisp. Serve in a separate little dish to accompany 1 l (2 pints) hot beef bouillon stock.

SEMOLINA DUMPLINGS
GRIESSNOCKERLN

30 g (1 oz) butter or margarine   water
1 egg   1 l (2 pints) brown beef bouillon
90 g (3 oz) coarse semolina   stock
salt

Cream the butter with the egg, gradually stir in the semolina and a pinch of salt. Cut out portions with a wet dessertspoon and immediately immerse in boiling salted water. Simmer in the covered pan for about 15 minutes. Drain, put in a tureen and cover with the beef stock just off the boil. Serve at once.

Soups

LIVER DUMPLINGS
LEBERKNÖDEL

120 g (4 oz) ox liver
45 g (1½ oz) white bread, soaked
  in water and squeezed well
a little finely chopped onion
finely chopped parsley
30 g (1 oz) fat

1 egg
30 g (1 oz) homemade
  breadcrumbs
salt, pepper, marjoram
1 l (2 pints) white beef bouillon
  stock

Scrape the liver with a blunt knife, discard skin and put with the bread through a sieve or mix in an electric blender. Soften the onion and parsley in the fat, and stir into the purée, together with the breadcrumbs, egg, salt, pepper and marjoram. Let the mixture stand in a cool place for about an hour. Scoop out small portions, lightly roll them into dumplings between the palms of the hands, immerse them carefully into the lightly boiling stock, cover the pan and simmer for 10 minutes. You can make larger dumplings to serve as a separate course accompanied by a salad. In this case the dumplings could be boiled in salted water or in vegetable stock.

CHICKEN BOUILLON
KLARE HÜHNERSUPPE

1 boiling fowl, or chicken joints,
  weight about 1½ kg (3 lb)
90 g (3 oz) each:
    carrots
    parsnip

90 g (3 oz) each:
  onion
  celery
2½ l (4 pints) slightly salted water

Put the chicken and the roughly chopped vegetables with cold water in a pan with a well-fitting lid, and boil steadily until tender. Drain into a bowl and when cold skim off the fat. The chicken meat can be used in a pâté or a risotto.

CHILLED CHICKEN BOUILLON
HÜHNERGELEESUPPE

1 l (2 pints) chicken bouillon
  (above)
30 g (1 oz) gelatine

finely chopped parsley
salt, pepper

If you use fresh stock, let it get cold and remove the fat. Bring it to the boil again, and dissolve the gelatine in some of the near-boiling stock. If the chicken bouillon has been made from bouillon cubes it will require the full 30 g (1 oz) amount of gelatine. Chicken bouillon made from whole chicken or chicken joints will jelly with only half the amount of gelatine added. Add to the remainder of the stock. Season. Let the jelly set, break it up with a fork and keep in the refrigerator for at least 1 hour before serving. Serve in individual bowls with parsley sprinkled over the top.

BEEF BOUILLON STOCK can be chilled in the same way.

CHICKEN BOUILLON WITH LIVER AND MUSHROOM GARNISH

KLARE HÜHNERSUPPE MIT LEBERN UND SCHWÄMMEN

1 l (2 pints) chicken bouillon (p. 15)   60 g (2 oz) butter
60 g (2 oz) chicken livers   salt, pepper
60 g (2 oz) mushrooms

Gently cook the sliced livers and mushrooms in the butter. Add salt and pepper. Bring the chicken stock to the boil, add the garnish and simmer for a minute.

CHICKEN GIBLET SOUP   HÜHNERKLEINSUPPE

1 kg (2 lb) chicken giblets   about 6 dl (1 pint) water
120 g (4 oz) each: 60 g (2 oz) chicken livers
    parsnip   60 g (2 oz) mushrooms
    celery   60 g (2 oz) butter
    carrots   60 g (2 oz) margarine
    onion   30 g (1 oz) flour
6 dl (1 pint) chicken bouillon   salt, pepper
  (p. 15)   chopped parsley

Bring the giblets and the roughly chopped vegetables to the boil in the chicken bouillon. Simmer steadily in the covered pan for 40 minutes, adding water as needed. Strain the stock into a bowl, chop the hearts and gizzards very small and reserve as garnish for the soup. Cook the extra 60 g (2 oz) sliced livers and mushrooms in the butter with a little salt and pepper, and reserve these, too, as garnish. Make a smooth sauce from the margarine, flour and stock. Season to taste. Add the garnishes and simmer for a few more moments. Serve sprinkled with chopped parsley.

CHICKEN PURÉE SOUP   HÜHNERPUREESUPPE

720 g (1½ lb) chicken joints
60 g (2 oz) each:
    carrots
    parsnip
    onion
    celery

105 g (3½ oz) margarine
60 g (2 oz) plain flour
1 yolk of egg lightly beaten with
    1 tablespoon milk
salt, pepper
1¾ l (3 pints) water

Boil the chicken and roughly chopped vegetables in slightly salted water in a covered pan until the meat is tender and comes easily off the bones. Drain and reserve the stock. Scrape the meat off the bones and put half the quantity through a sieve or liquidize in an electric blender. Cut the remaining meat into very small neat pieces and reserve as garnish for the soup. Make a smooth sauce from the margarine, flour and stock. Stir the egg and milk mixture, and then the thickened stock, into the meat purée. Add the meat garnish and seasoning. Reheat but do *not* allow the soup to boil once the egg has been added.

GOULASH SOUP   GULASCHSUPPE

This soup is eaten in Vienna at all hours, particularly for elevenses and at four or five in the morning after an all-night party.

120 g (4 oz) onion, cut into fine
    rings
1 clove of garlic, crushed
240 g (8 oz) shin of beef
60 g (2 oz) fat or dripping
1 tablespoon paprika
1 teaspoon marjoram

1 teaspoon caraway seed
30 g (1 oz) flour
salt
1 dessertspoon vinegar
1 l (2 pints) water, or vegetable
    stock
120 g (4 oz) potatoes, optional

Soups

Soften the onion and garlic in the fat. Push to one side and add the meat diced small, together with the salt and spices. Turn over low heat until the meat is brown all over. Dust with the flour and stir for a few more moments. Gradually add vinegar and the water or vegetable stock, bring to the boil while stirring and simmer steadily in a covered pan until the meat is soft. Taste, and add more seasonings, if necessary. Peeled potatoes diced very small can be added to the soup when the meat is nearly cooked.

CLEAR OXTAIL SOUP

KLARE OCHSENSCHLEPPSUPPE

480 g (1 lb) oxtail
240 g (8 oz) beef bones
60 g (2 oz) each:
    parsnip
    carrots
    celery
    onion
90 g (3 oz) fat
1 l (2 pints) water

salt, pepper

For the garnish:
60 g (2 oz) boiled peas
60 g (2 oz) boiled beans, sliced small
60 g (2 oz) sliced mushrooms cooked in a little butter

Gently fry the chopped root vegetables, onion and celery in the fat. Push to one side and add the oxtail, cut into pieces, the crushed bones, and seasoning. Continue frying until the meat is lightly browned all over. Add water and boil in a covered pan until the meat is soft, from 2 to 3 hours. Drain into a bowl, discard bones and vegetables, scrape the meat off the oxtail. Cut up very small and set aside with the other garnishes. Season further to taste, and add a bouillon cube if no bones have been used. Allow the broth to get cold, preferably overnight, in order to skim off all the fat. Then, before serving, add the garnishes and bring to the boil.

SEMOLINA SOUP

GRIESS-SUPPE

30 g (1 oz) fat or dripping
90 g (3 oz) coarse semolina

1 l (2 pints) brown beef stock (p. 12)

Gently fry the semolina in the fat over a low heat. Pour on the

18

stock while stirring. Simmer in a covered pan for about 5 minutes.
Add salt and pepper to taste.

CABBAGE SOUP   KRAUTSUPPE

240 g (8 oz) white cabbage,
   shredded
60 g (2 oz) onion, shredded
120 g (4 oz) fat or dripping

60 g (2 oz) flour
1 l (2 pints) brown beef stock
   (p. 12)
salt, pepper

Soften the cabbage and onion in the fat over low heat. Dust with
flour, and stir and cook for a few more moments. Pour on the stock
and boil steadily in a covered pan until the cabbage is tender. Add
salt and pepper. To make this soup a meal in itself, add a pair of
frankfurter sausages, cut into rounds and simmered in the soup for
a few moments. Or add 120 g (4 oz) diced cooked gammon to the
soup.

CARROT SOUP   KAROTTENSUPPE

240 g (8 oz) carrots
chopped parsley
90 g (3 oz) margarine
1 teaspoon sugar

60 g (2 oz) flour
1 teaspoon lemon juice
1 l (2 pints) water
salt, pepper

Cook the grated carrots and parsley gently in the margarine. Stir
in the sugar, salt and pepper and cook a little longer over a low heat.
Add the flour and stir for a minute. Stir in the lemon juice, add the
water and bring to the boil, stirring until smooth. Season further if
needed. Simmer in a covered pan until the carrots are soft, stirring
occasionally.

ASPARAGUS SOUP   SPARGELSUPPE

480 g (1 lb) cheapest asparagus
90 g (3 oz) butter or margarine
60 g (2 oz) flour

1 l (2 pints) white beef bouillon
   stock (p. 11)
salt, pepper

Scrape the asparagus stems and cut off the woody ends. Boil the asparagus in a little salted water until tender. Drain, and reserve the stock. Cut the stems into 1 cm ($\frac{1}{2}$ in) lengths. Leave the heads whole, and set both aside as garnish for the soup. Make a roux from butter and flour, pour on some of the asparagus stock and bring to the boil while stirring. Stir and boil to dissolve all lumps. Add the beef stock and the remainder of the asparagus stock. Add salt and pepper to taste. Transfer the asparagus heads and stems to the soup, bring to the boil and simmer for a minute before serving.

CHIVES SOUP   SCHNITTLAUCHSUPPE

60 g (2 oz) finely chopped chives
120 g (4 oz) margarine
60 g (2 oz) flour
1 l (2 pints) brown beef bouillon
stock (p. 12)

120 g (4 oz) potatoes
salt, pepper
1 egg beaten with a little milk

Fry the chives gently in the margarine. Continuing over a low heat, stir in the flour and cook for a few moments. Add the stock, bring to the boil and stir until smooth. Add the peeled potatoes diced very small, and cook until tender. Just before serving bring the soup to the boil, remove from the heat and stir in the egg. The soup must *not* boil once the egg has been added. Add salt and pepper to taste.

GARLIC SOUP   KNOBLAUCHSUPPE

30 g (1 oz) garlic, about 7 sections
60 g (2 oz) onion
45 g (1½ oz) fat or dripping
1 l (2 pints) white beef bouillon

stock (p. 11), or bouillon cubes
dissolved in water
salt, pepper

Fry the crushed garlic and the very finely chopped onion in the fat, over a low heat, until golden brown. Add the beef stock, salt and pepper and simmer in a covered pan for 10 minutes. Before serving put thin slices of toasted white bread at the bottom of the tureen or in each bowl.

HARICOT BEAN SOUP   WEISSE BOHNENSUPPE

150 g (5 oz) dried haricot beans,   *finely chopped parsley*
  soaked overnight   *crushed garlic*
1 l (2 pints) water, or vegetable   *60 g (2 oz) fat or dripping*
  stock   *30 g (1 oz) flour*
30 g (1 oz) finely chopped onion   *salt, pepper*

Boil the beans in the water or stock until soft—this will take a long
time, perhaps 2 hours. Strain into a bowl. Soften the onion, parsley
and garlic in the fat. Dust with the flour, sprinkle in salt and pepper
and continue to stir for a minute. Add the bean stock and bring to
the boil while stirring. Pass the sauce and the beans through a sieve
or mix in an electric blender. Add the rest of the stock. Season to
taste.

Add 120 g (4 oz) cooked, diced bacon or ham to the soup to make
HARICOT BEAN AND BACON SOUP, which is very substantial.

GREEN LENTIL SOUP   LINSENSUPPE

150 g (5 oz) large continental   *60 g (2 oz) fat*
  lentils   *60 g (2 oz) flour*
30 g (1 oz) finely chopped onion   *1 dessertspoon vinegar*
finely chopped parsley   *1 teaspoon sugar*
30 g (1 oz) fat or dripping   *salt, pepper*
1 l (2 pints) vegetable stock or
  water

Wash the lentils in a large sieve under the cold tap. Spread out on a
tray and discard any little stones and pieces of wood. Put the lentils
into cold water or stock. Bring to the boil and cook until soft.
Meanwhile soften the onion and parsley in 30 g (1 oz) fat. Strain the
lentil stock into a bowl and pass the lentils through a sieve or blend
in a liquidizer, together with the onion and parsley. Make a sauce
from the fat, flour, salt, pepper, sugar, vinegar and stock. Stir into
the lentil purée, season further if needed; reheat and stir for a few
minutes until the soup is smooth.

Soups

ONION SOUP

360 g (12 oz) onion
60 g (2 oz) fat, dripping or
margarine

60 g (2 oz) flour
1 l (2 pints) white beef stock (p. 11)
salt, pepper

Slice the onions finely and lightly brown in the fat over a low heat. Dust with the flour and continue frying a little longer. Pour on the stock, bring to the boil while stirring, add salt and pepper and boil gently in a covered pan for 10 minutes. Allow 2 half-slices of French loaf or white crusty bread for each serving and put these in the soup tureen or individual bowls before adding the soup.

ONION AND POTATO SOUP

ZWIEBEL-UND KARTOFFELSUPPE

240 g (8 oz) onion
45 g (1½ oz) fat, dripping or
margarine
45 g (1½ oz) flour
1 tablespoon vinegar

1½ l (2½ pints) brown beef stock
(p. 12)
120 g (4 oz) potatoes
salt, pepper
1 dl (4 oz) sour cream (optional)

Over a low heat lightly brown the finely sliced onion in the fat, dust with the flour and cook for a few more moments. Add vinegar and stock and bring to the boil while stirring. Add the peeled potatoes diced small. Cook in the covered pan until the potatoes are soft. Add salt and pepper to taste. If you wish, stir in 1 dl (4 oz) sour cream, and sprinkle a little chopped parsley or chives over the top.

GREEN PEA AND LETTUCE SOUP

FEINE ERBSENSUPPE

This is a soup for special occasions; the quantities will provide for 10 servings.

500 g (1 lb) shelled green peas
2 medium size cos lettuces

parsley
5½ dl (1 pint) slightly salted water

2½ l (4 pints) chicken bouillon
 (p. 15) or white beef bouillon
 stock (p. 11)

2½ dl (½ pint) double cream
120 g (4 oz) butter
salt, pepper

Boil the roughly chopped cos lettuces, the peas and parsely in 6 dl (1 pint) slightly salted water until tender. Reserve about 60 g (2 oz) of the cooked peas as a garnish for the soup and reserve the stock. Pass the remainder of the vegetables through a sieve or mix in an electric blender. Stir the purée into the vegetable stock and the bouillon, add the butter and bring to the boil while stirring. Season to taste. Simmer for about 5 minutes, stirring frequently. Before serving stir in the cream, add the reserved peas and bring almost to the boil.

You can make a PEA POD SOUP (SCHOTENSUPPE) for no extra cost if you boil the pods of really young peas in salted water, sieve or liquidize them, and add the purée to a sauce made from their stock and 2 parts butter to 1 part flour, add salt and pepper to taste. Simmer for 10 minutes.

SALSIFY SOUP

SCHWARZWURZELSUPPE

480 g (1 lb) salsify
90 g (3 oz) margarine
60 g (2 oz) flour

1 l (2 pints) water
salt

Scrape the salsify and, to prevent discolouration, immediately immerse in the slightly salted cold water. Boil in a covered pan until soft. Make a sauce with the margarine, flour and vegetable stock. Bring to the boil while stirring, and cook for a few moments. Sieve the salsify into the sauce, or blend both in a liquidizer. Taste, add salt if needed. Reheat and stir for a minute or two.

JERUSALEM ARTICHOKE SOUP (TOPINAMBURSUPPE) is made by the same method.

SAUERKRAUT SOUP I   SAUERKRAUTSUPPE I

240 g (8 oz) gammon in one piece	*240 g (8 oz) sauerkraut*
	30 g (1 oz) flour
60 g (2 oz) fat bacon rashers	*1 l (2 pints) brown beef stock (p. 12)*

Boil the gammon until soft, drain, and cut into small dice. Reserve. Cut the bacon rashers into small pieces and cook over low heat until just soft. Push to one side, put in the sauerkraut and stir for about 3 minutes. Dust with the flour, and cook and stir everything for about a minute. Add the stock, the diced gammon and seasoning to taste. Bring to the boil while stirring. Simmer in the covered pan for a few minutes. This soup is very substantial; it makes a one-course meal on its own.

Shredded Dutch cabbage can be substituted for the sauerkraut in both Sauerkraut Soups to make CABBAGE SOUP AND BACON. When using fresh cabbage a little fat or dripping may have to be added to the fat extracted from the bacon rashers in order to soften the shredded cabbage for about 5 minutes. A little vinegar will have to be added to the seasoning.

SAUERKRAUT SOUP II   SAUERKRAUTSUPPE II

This is a very solid soup.

60 g (2 oz) fat bacon rashers	*15 g (½ oz) flour*
240 g (8 oz) sauerkraut	*1 pair frankfurter sausages*
30 g (1 oz) fat or dripping	*1 l (2 pints) brown beef stock (p. 12)*

Gently fry the bacon, diced small, over a low heat. Push to one side and add the sauerkraut. Continue cooking, adding a little stock if needed. Make a sauce from fat, flour and some of the stock, stirring to dissolve all lumps. Immerse the frankfurter sausages in boiling water, take off the heat and leave them in the water for 5 minutes. Drain, and slice into 1 cm (½ in) rounds. Transfer them to the sauce, together with the remainder of the stock and the sauerkraut. Add salt and pepper if needed.

SPINACH SOUP

480 g (1 lb) spinach
1 clove garlic
90 g (3 oz) margarine

60 g (2 oz) flour
salt, pepper
1 l (2 pints) water

Thoroughly wash and drain the spinach, and boil with a very little added water until tender. Drain into a bowl. Fry the crushed garlic in the margarine, add salt and pepper, dust with the flour and stir for a moment. Pour on the spinach stock and bring to the boil while stirring. Add the spinach and pass through a sieve, or mix in an electric blender. Add water to bring up to the required quantity, taste, and add seasoning and a bouillon cube as required. An egg beaten with ½ dl (2 oz) single cream or top of the milk can be stirred into the slightly cooled soup, but do not allow to boil once the egg has been added.

PARADISE (TOMATO) SOUP

120 g (4 oz) margarine
480 g (1 lb) ripe tomatoes
30 g (1 oz) flour
1 dessertspoon sugar

1 dessertspoon vinegar
salt, pepper
8¼ dl (1¼ pints) water

Melt the margarine over a low heat and soften the roughly cut tomatoes. Stir in flour, sugar, vinegar, salt and pepper and continue stirring and cooking for a few moments. Add the water and boil in a covered pan until the tomatoes are very soft. Pass through a sieve or put in an electric blender. Bring to the boil before serving.

COLD PARADISE SOUP (TOMATO)

The soup can be made with fresh or tinned tomatoes. When using fresh tomatoes scald and peel 480 g (1 lb) before simmering in 6 dl (1 pint) slightly salted water until soft. Pass through a sieve or an electric blender. Dissolve 30 g (1 oz) of gelatine in a little of the very hot liquid, add the rest of the purée and the remainder of the liquid, with salt, pepper, vinegar and sugar to taste. Let the soup set, and serve cold in individual bowls. Decorate with a few thin slices of cucumber.

SPRING VEGETABLE SOUP — FRÜHLINGSSUPPE

1½ (2½ pints) white beef bouillon
    stock (p. 11)
60 g (2 oz) each:
    finely shredded white
      cabbage
    carrots, diced small
    runner beans, finely sliced

60 g (2 oz) each:
    sprigs of cauliflower
    peas
    sliced mushrooms, cooked
      in 30 g (1 oz)
      margarine
salt, pepper

Cook the carrots in the boiling stock in a covered pan for about 10 minutes. Add the beans, cauliflower and cabbage, and when the vegetables are nearly tender add the peas and boil for a few more minutes. Add the cooked mushrooms, and season to taste.

WATERCRESS SOUP — KRESSESUPPE

1 or 2 bundles watercress, about
    240 g (8 oz)
90 g (3 oz) margarine
30 g (1 oz) flour

salt, pepper
1 l (2 pints) white beef bouillon
    stock (p. 11)
¼ dl (2 oz) sour cream

Cut off the stems and gently fry the chopped cress in the margarine over a low heat. Dust with the flour, add salt and pepper and continue cooking gently for a few moments. Pour in the stock, bring to the boil while stirring and simmer in the covered pan for about 5 minutes. Just before serving bring the soup to the boil and stir in the sour cream.

Hors d'Oeuvre,
Lunch and Supper Dishes

Many of the recipes in this section are useful as a main-course dish, with vegetables and a sauce added, while many of them make good, one-course lunches and suppers. I reserve the soufflés for family meals only, because soufflés need very exact cooking and serving times which do not allow for late guests or for lingering over drinks. Pâtés, moulds, jellies and all the other cold dishes are particularly suitable as hors d'oeuvre for a dinner party, although I also often serve them for family lunches or suppers at the weekend.

Cold Pâtés, Mousses and Moulds

CHICKEN PÂTÉ
Serves 10

HÜHNERPASTETE

1 small chicken or separate joints, about ½ kg–1 kg (1–2 lb)

90 g (3 oz) each:
    carrots
    parsnip
    celery

120 g (4 oz) stale white bread, soaked in a little milk

120 g (4 oz) sliced mushrooms

90 g (3 oz) finely chopped onion

90 g (3 oz) margarine

2 eggs

about 180 g (6 oz) rashers of fat bacon

salt, pepper, grated nutmeg, marjoram

Boil the chicken and the roughly chopped root vegetables and celery in salted water—use as little water as possible—until the meat comes easily off the bones. Strain into a bowl. (Use the stock and vegetables for a soup.) Chop the meat very small or put it through a mincer or an electric blender, together with the bread, squeezed out. Cook the onion and mushrooms gently in the margarine and add to the minced meat. Stir in the beaten eggs, salt and pepper and spices to taste. Transfer the pâté mixture to a bread tin lined with bacon rashers, cover with the remaining bacon rashers. Cover the top of the tin with baking foil, stand in a bain-marie of cold water and bake in a moderate oven for $2\frac{1}{2}$ to 3 hours. Allow the pâté to cool in the tin before turning out. Keep in the refrigerator for several hours before serving.

HARE PÂTÉ

4 legs of hare	*finely chopped parsley*
90 g (3 oz) each:	*30 g (1 oz) fat*
carrots	*120 g (4 oz) mushrooms, diced*
parsnip	*2 eggs*
1 tablespoon wine vinegar	*120 g (4 oz) bacon, diced*
few peppercorns	*salt, pepper*
60 g (2 oz) stale white bread,	*mixed herbs*
soaked in water	*120 g (4 oz) rashers of fat bacon*
30 g (1 oz) finely chopped onion	

Boil the hare in salted water, to which the vinegar and a few peppercorns have been added, until it comes easily off the bone. Use as little water as possible. Strain. Scrape the meat off the bones and put it, together with the squeezed-out bread, through a mincer, or in an electric blender, or chop it very small. Soften the onion and parsley in the fat, and stir into the minced hare, together with the bread, diced mushrooms and bacon, eggs, and seasonings to taste. Line a bread tin with bacon rashers, fill it with the pâté mixture, place bacon rashers on top, cover with baking foil, stand in a bain-marie of cold water and bake in a moderate oven for about $2\frac{1}{2}$ hours, or until the pâté has set. Allow the pâté to cool before turning out; when cold enough transfer to the refrigerator. Serve with Cranberry Sauce.

HARLEQUIN PÂTÉ (MEAT PÂTÉ) HARLEKINBRATEN

480 g (1 lb) minced beef
60 g (2 oz) white bread, soaked
  in water
120 g (4 oz) cooked ham or
  tongue, diced small
120 g (4 oz) gherkins, diced
  small

2 eggs
2 hard-boiled eggs
salt, pepper, marjoram
about 180 g (6 oz) rashers of fat
  bacon

Squeeze the bread thoroughly and stir together with the minced meat, the gherkins, the cooked ham, the raw eggs, and seasonings to taste. Line a bread tin with bacon rashers and fill with the pâté mixture. Insert the peeled hard-boiled eggs into the mixture, taking care to cover them completely. Cover the top of the pâté with bacon, and cover the top of the tin with baking foil. Bake in a bain-marie of cold water in a moderate oven for about 2 hours, when the mixture should have fully set. Allow the pâté to cool before turning out. Keep in the refrigerator for several hours before serving.

PARTRIDGE OR PHEASANT PÂTÉ
REBHUN–ODER FASANENPASTETE

Follow the recipe for Chicken Pâté (p. 27), but instead of soaking the bread in milk, soak it in red wine or in a substitute made from wine vinegar, water and sugar, mixed to taste.

CHICKEN MOULD HÜHNERGELEE

1 chicken or separate joints, about
  1½ kg (3 lb)
120 g (4 oz) each:
  onion
  carrot
  celery

1 l (2 pints) water
60 g (2 oz) sliced mushrooms
  cooked in 15 g (½ oz) margarine
60 g (2 oz) boiled peas
2 hard-boiled eggs, sliced
15 g (½ oz) gelatine

Put the chopped onion and celery and sliced carrots into cold salted water, bring to the boil and add the chicken. Boil in the covered pan until the meat comes easily off the bone. Strain into a bowl. Dissolve the gelatine in the very hot stock, scrape the meat off the bones and cut into neat pieces. Taste the stock, re-season as necessary and transfer to a basin rinsed out with cold water and large enough to take both the stock and the meat and garnishes. Stand until the stock *starts* to set, then stir in the meat, the carrots, mushrooms and peas and sliced eggs. As soon as the mould is cold enough, put it in the refrigerator and let it set firm. Turn out on to a serving dish and keep cold until ready to serve.

FISH MOULD   GESULZTER FISCH

Steam fillets of white fish in a little salted water. Strain into a bowl. Flake the fish, pour on the fish stock with enough additional water or vegetable stock to cover the flaked fish. Dissolve one or two bouillon cubes to add flavour to the stock. Strain into a measuring jug and dissolve enough gelatine, according to makers' instructions, in the hot stock to make a jelly. Line a basin, large enough to hold the stock and fish, with sliced tomato and cucumber. Carefully pour in the stock. Sprinkle with chopped parsley. When the jelly *starts* setting fold in the flaked fish. Let the mould set in the refrigerator. Turn out on to a serving dish, and keep cold until ready to serve. Serve with homemade mayonnaise.

HAM MOUSSE   SCHINKENCREME

480 g (1 lb) boiled ham or lean gammon	*3 eggs, separated*
	finely chopped parsley
90 g (3 oz) stale white bread, soaked in a little milk	*1 dl (4 oz) double cream*
	salt, pepper
90 g (3 oz) margarine	

Put the ham through a mincer or chop it very small. Put it through a sieve or in an electric blender, together with the squeezed-out bread. Cream the margarine with the egg yolks and stir them into the meat purée. Stir in the parsley and whipped cream, then season to taste, and finally fold in the stiffly beaten whites of egg. Transfer the mixture to a greased and floured pudding basin, secure the top and steam for 1 hour. Turn out, and serve hot or cold with Cranberry Sauce (p. 102) or Cumberland Sauce (p. 103).

Light Savoury Dishes

STUFFED BREAD LOAF JÄGERWECKEN

1 white sandwich loaf, uncut
150 g (5 oz) butter
concentrated anchovy paste
180 g (6 oz) cooked ham or
    gammon

180 g (6 oz) cooked tongue
120 (4 oz) gherkins
180 g (6 oz) Edam cheese

Cut the crust about 1 cm (½ in) thick off one end of the loaf. This will be the lid of the stuffed loaf. Scoop out the bread as thoroughly as possible, taking care not to pierce the crust. Cream the butter with enough concentrated anchovy to give a strong flavour. Stir in ham, tongue, gherkins and cheese all diced very small. If the mixture lacks firmness stir in some crumbs from the scooped-out bread. Pack the mixture well into the loaf, put on the lid and roll up tightly in a clean dry teacloth. Tie firmly with string and leave in the refrigerator for 24 hours. Cut into 1 cm (½ in) slices to serve.

SAVOURY PANCAKES PALATSCHINKEN PIKANT GEFÜLLT

Make 2 pancakes per person. Keep them hot on an inverted saucer in a slow oven or in your cooker's warming drawer. Cover with foil to prevent drying out. Make the filling, for example:

boiled or roast chicken, chopped
    small
or scrambled brains
or spinach, boiled in salted water
    and chopped
or sliced mushrooms cooked in
    butter

or steamed, fresh or frozen
    prawns or shrimps
or chopped cooked ham and
    grated Emmental or Gruyère
    cheese

31

The filling is coated with a thick white sauce, made from 1 part butter or margarine, 2 parts flour, and milk or sour cream or single cream, and salt and pepper. Spoon some filling in the centre of each pancake, roll up the pancake and pack them in a greased ovenproof dish. Pour the remainder of the sauce over them, sprinkle with homemade breadcrumbs, dot with flakes of butter and put in a moderately hot oven for about 15 minutes, until the top bubbles and is lightly browned. Serve very hot.

PASTA AND CHOPPED HAM   SCHINKENFLECKERLN

Small squares of pasta are used in the Viennese recipe, but any other small pasta can be used. Boil 480 g (1 lb) pasta in salted water, drain into a colander and very quickly douse under the cold tap. Into the hot pasta lightly stir 120 g (4 oz) melted butter and 180–240 g (6–8 oz) diced cooked ham or gammon.

SAUSAGE BASKETS   WURSTSCHÜSSERLN

240 g (8 oz) extrawurst sausage (see below)	480 g (1 lb) spinach, boiled and drained
60 g (2 oz) fat	1 egg for each slice of sausage
	salt

The extrawurst should be cut into 5 mm (¼ in) slices and it is essential the skin should be left on. Fry the slices on one side only in the fat. They will curl at the edges and form either little cups or domes. Fill with the hot chopped spinach, mixed with a little butter. Place a fried egg on top of each and serve at once.

Instead of spinach, mushrooms cooked in butter, or scrambled eggs, can be used as a filling. If you can't find extrawurst, Polish ham sausage could be used—it should be 7–10 cm (3–4 in) in diameter.

SAVOURY CUPS   PIKANTE TEIGKÖRBCHEN

135 g (4½ oz) flour	1 tablespoon sour cream
90 g (3 oz) margarine	salt

Work the ingredients into a dough. Rest in a cool place for ½ hour. Roll out about 5 mm (¼ in) thick. Cut into rounds to fit cup cake or bun tins. Line the tins with pastry and press down the edges lightly with a fork. Bake blind—with, for example, dried beans—in a moderate oven for about 15 minutes. Remove the beans and return to the oven for another 5 minutes. Serve with the fillings suggested for Savoury Pancakes (p. 31).

SAVOURY VOL-AU-VENT

VOL-AU-VENT PIKANT GEFÜLLT

480 g (1 lb) bought puff pastry will make 8 to 10 vol-au-vents. Roll out the pastry 5 mm (¼ in) thick and cut into rounds with a 7½ cm (3 in) pastry cutter. Cut into half the number of rounds again, with a 5 cm (2 in) cutter, forming rings. Damp the uncut rounds with water and place a pastry ring on each. Place these, and the 5 cm (2 in) rounds which will be the lids, on a dampened baking sheet. Bake in a hot oven for about 15 minutes, until the pastry has risen and is golden brown. Fill the pastry cases with any of the fillings suggested for Savoury Pancakes (p. 31). Put a pastry lid on each vol-au-vent case and serve hot.

If you wish, allow the pastry to get cold and fill with crab, shrimps or vegetable salad, all coated with homemade mayonnaise.

SAVOURY SPONGE ROLL

PIKANTE BISKUITROLLE

4 flat tablespoons self-raising flour

4 eggs, separated
salt
60 g (2 oz) homemade mayonnaise

90–120 g (3–4 oz) thinly sliced ham
90–120 g (3–4 oz) thinly sliced Gruyère or Emmental cheese
60 g (2 oz) chopped gherkins

Beat the yolks until frothy, stir in the flour and a little salt. Fold in the stiffly beaten whites. Spread the mixture about 1 cm (½ in) thick on a greased and floured Swiss roll tin, lined with greaseproof paper, and bake in a moderately hot oven for about 15 minutes, until the sponge is very lightly browned and comes easily off the

B

paper. While the sponge is baking, prepare the mayonnaise and fillings ready for immediate use. Turn the baked sponge on to a wooden board. Quickly spread with mayonnaise, on which the ham and cheese are placed in no more than 2 layers. Sprinkle with the chopped gherkins and quickly roll up like a Swiss roll. Wrap the roll tightly in a clean dry teacloth and tie up. Leave the wrapped roll overnight in the refrigerator. Serve cut into slices about 1 cm (½ in) thick.

Egg Dishes

EGGS ON CHEESE KÄSE UND EI

Grease individual fireproof dishes or cocottes and place in each a piece of Gruyère or Emmental cheese, about 1 cm (½ in) thick and large enough to cover the bottom of the cocotte. Put under a hot grill, or on the top shelf of a very hot oven, until the cheese starts to melt. This should take about 2 or 3 minutes. Remove the cocottes from the oven and place a whole raw egg in each, on top of the cheese. Gently pour a very little melted butter over each egg and return the dishes to the oven or under the grill until the eggs have set—2 or 3 minutes.

STUFFED HARD-BOILED EGGS GEFÜLLTE EIER

6 hard-boiled eggs	*chopped parsley*
60 g (2 oz) butter or margarine	*15 g (½ oz) capers*
1 teaspoon French mustard	*concentrated anchovy paste*

Halve the eggs horizontally and carefully scoop out the yolks. Cream with butter until fluffy and stir in enough anchovy paste to give a strong flavour. Add a little salt if needed. Pipe or spoon into the hollow egg whites. Decorate with capers and parsley. Keep in a cold place for at least 1 hour before serving. To make the eggs stand in the serving dish cut a tiny slice from the bottom of each egg.

EGG MAYONNAISE SALAD EIERMAYONNAISE SALAT

5 hard-boiled eggs
2½ dl (½ pint) homemade
mayonnaise
240 g (8 oz) firm boiled potatoes
240 g (8 oz) tomatoes
60 g (2 oz) inner stick of celery

60 g (2 oz) cooked ham or
gammon
60 g (2 oz) shelled walnuts
parsley
chives

Halve and slice the tomatoes, cut the celery into small pieces, dice the ham and potatoes and chop the nuts. Coat all these ingredients with mayonnaise, reserving about a tablespoon for decorating the eggs. Spoon the mayonnaise mixture into a serving dish, place the eggs on top and decorate them with mayonnaise sprinkled with chopped parsley and chives. Keep in a cold place until ready to serve.

PEASANTS' OMELETTE BAUERNOMELETTE

120 g (4 oz) streaky bacon
90 g (3 oz) onion
parsley
120 g (4 oz) fat

240 g (8 oz) potatoes, boiled,
peeled and diced
12 eggs
salt, pepper

Gently fry the finely chopped onion and parsley with the diced bacon in some fat. Whisk the eggs lightly with salt and pepper and stir in the onion, parsley, bacon and potatoes. From this mixture, quickly fry six omelettes in hot fat. Fold each omelette in half and serve at once. You can substitute any other cooked or left-over vegetables, such as peas, runner beans, leeks, carrots or cauliflower.

SPINACH OMELETTE SPINATOMELETTE

480 g (1 lb) spinach (about 300 g
(10 oz) frozen)
4 eggs, separated

120 g (4 oz) sliced mushrooms,
cooked in a little butter
salt, pepper

Cook the washed spinach in as little water as possible, drain and make a purée. Beat the egg yolks lightly with salt and pepper and stir into the spinach purée. Then fold in the stiffly beaten whites of egg. Fry like an omelette. Spread one half of the omelette with the cooked mushrooms, fold the other half over, lift carefully out of the pan and serve at once. Alternatively fill the omelette with scrambled eggs. A hot Cheese Sauce (p. 101) can be served separately.

EGGS IN SOUR CREAM I   RAHMEIER I

120 g (4 oz) sliced mushrooms   *1 dl (4 oz) sour cream*
parsley   *5 hard-boiled eggs*
60 g (2 oz) butter or margarine   *breadcrumbs*
30 g (1 oz) flour   *salt, pepper*
30 g (1 oz) cold water

Cook the sliced mushrooms and the chopped parsley gently in the butter, stir in the flour and cook over a low heat for a few more moments. Pour on the cold water, increase the heat a little and boil for a minute, stirring continuously. Stir in the sour cream and bring just to the point of boiling. Season to taste. Place the eggs, halved lengthways, in a shallow, greased ovenproof dish, large enough for the eggs to lie in one layer. Pour over the sauce, sprinkle lightly with homemade breadcrumbs and dot with flakes of butter. Put in a hot oven for 5 to 10 minutes, until the top bubbles and is lightly browned.

EGGS IN SOUR CREAM II   RAHMEIER II

2½ dl (½ pint) sour cream   *chopped parsley*
10 eggs   *chopped chives*
3 anchovy fillets, tinned or   *breadcrumbs*
  salted, chopped small

Grease a shallow ovenproof dish and pour the sour cream evenly over the bottom. Slip in the raw eggs. Cover the eggs with the chopped anchovy, parsley and chives. Sprinkle with homemade breadcrumbs and dot with butter flakes. Put the dish for about 3 minutes in a very hot oven, until the eggs are soft boiled and the top is lightly browned.

SPINACH ROLL   SPINATROULADE

480 g (1 lb) spinach (about 300 g   salt and pepper
   (10 oz) frozen)   5 eggs scrambled in 60 g (2 oz)
4 eggs, separated   butter, for the filling
flour as needed

Cook the thoroughly washed spinach in as little water as possible, drain and make a purée. Add the egg yolks, with salt and pepper, to the purée and stir in about a fistful of flour to give the mixture body. Fold in the stiffly beaten whites and spread the mixture about 5 mm (¼ in) thick on a greased and floured Swiss-roll tin. Bake in a hot oven for about 15 minutes, until the omelette has risen and is firm on top. Turn out, quickly spread with the scrambled eggs, and roll up like a Swiss roll. Serve at once with Cheese Sauce (p. 101) or with a salad.

Cheese Dishes

CHEESE FLAN   KÄSETORTE

For the pastry: For the filling:
120 g (4 oz) margarine   ¼ dl (2 oz) milk
120 g (4 oz) flour   60 g (2 oz) grated Parmesan,
90 g (3 oz) grated Parmesan,   Gruyère, Emmental or
   Gruyère, Emmental or   Cheddar cheese
   Cheddar cheese   15 g (½ oz) cornflour
salt   1 egg
                                  salt, pepper

Work the pastry ingredients into a dough. Roll out to fit an 18 cm (7 in) cake tin, but keep back enough dough to roll into a sausage about 1 cm (½ in) thick and long enough to circle the base of the flan. Press this lightly against the side of the tin, making a wall for the flan. Bake blind for 15 minutes in a moderate oven, when it should be half baked. Beat together the milk, cheese, cornflour, and salt and pepper to taste, and fill the flan with the mixture. Return to

37

the oven for another 10 to 15 minutes, or until the cheese custard has set and the pastry is firm to the touch. Eat hot or cold. The filling can be varied by substituting for the cheese cooked chopped ham, or cooked sliced mushrooms or shrimps.

CHEESE TARTLETS

KÄSETORTELETTEN

For the pastry:
120 g (4 oz) margarine
120 g (4 oz) plain flour
90 g (3 oz) grated cheese
salt

For the filling:
1 dl (4 oz) double cream
30 g (1 oz) grated Parmesan or Cheddar cheese
75 g (2½ oz) butter
3 egg yolks
salt, pepper, grated nutmeg

Work the pastry ingredients quickly and lightly into a dough. Roll out about 5 mm (¼ in) thick, cut into rounds with a 7½ cm (3 in) pastry cutter, and bake on a dampened baking sheet in a moderate oven for about 15 minutes, or until the pastry feels firm to the touch. Meanwhile make the filling by beating the ingredients over steam to a very thick custard. When the custard is completely cold spread it thickly on half the number of pastry rounds and put the other half on top.

MACARONI AND HAM AU GRATIN

GRATINIERTE MAKARONI

480 (1 lb) marcaroni, broken into 5 cm (2 in) pieces
120 g (4 oz) diced boiled ham or gammon
1 dl (4 oz) sour cream
2 eggs

120 g (4 oz) grated Parmesan or Cheddar cheese
30 g (1 oz) butter
30 g (1 oz) homemade bread-crumbs

Instead of macaroni, small shells, wheels or other suitable pasta can be used. Boil the pasta in salted water, drain, and quickly douse under the cold tap. Put a layer of pasta in a greased soufflé dish. Cover with a layer of ham and continue in layers, finishing with pasta. Stir together the sour cream, eggs, cheese, and salt and pepper to taste. Pour the sauce evenly over the last layer of pasta, sprinkle with breadcrumbs, dot with flakes of butter and put in a hot oven for about 10 minutes, until bubbling and lightly browned.

SEMOLINA PATTIES RÖMISCHE GRIESSCHEIBEN

6 dl (1 pint) milk
90 g (3 oz) margarine
240 g (8 oz) coarse semolina
pinch of salt

150 g (5 oz) grated Parmesan
cheese (or Emmental, Gruyère
or Cheddar)
1 egg
salt, pepper

Bring the slightly salted milk to the boil with the butter. Lower the heat a little and sprinkle in the semolina, stirring all the time. Boil and stir until the mixture is very thick. Remove from the heat and stir in the grated 90 g (3 oz) cheese. When cool enough, stir in the beaten egg. Add salt and pepper to taste. Transfer the mixture to a cold smooth surface—stone is best, but enamel, a baking sheet or Formica will do. Pat down lightly to about $1\frac{1}{2}$ cm ($\frac{3}{4}$ in) thickness, and leave the mixture to rest under a cloth wrung out in cold water, for about $\frac{1}{2}$ hour. Cut into rounds with a pastry cutter, roughly 4 cm ($1\frac{1}{2}$ in). Grease a shallow, wide ovenproof dish in which the rounds can be laid, overlapping as little as possible. Sprinkle them with the remaining 60 g (2 oz) grated cheese, dot with flakes of butter and put in a moderately hot oven, on a high shelf, for about 15 minutes, when the top should be nicely browned and bubbling. Alternatively cook under the grill: start with medium hot temperature and turn to hot when the patties have been heated through and need browning. Serve as soon as possible with Hot Tomato Sauce (p. 105).

FRIED CHEESE ON BREAD GEBACKENE KÄSEBRÖTCHEN

1 French stick of bread
45 g ($1\frac{1}{2}$ oz) margarine
120 g (4 oz) grated Gruyère,
Emmental or Cheddar cheese

30 g (1 oz) flour
1 egg
salt, paprika

Cream the margarine with the cheese, stir in the egg, the flour, and salt and paprika to taste. Cut the bread into 1 cm (½ in) thick slices, spread thickly with the mixture and deep-fry in hot fat or oil until golden brown. Serve as soon as possible with a lettuce salad.

CHEESE FRIED IN BREADCRUMBS

GEBACKENER EMMENTALER

Allow 120 g (4 oz) of Emmental or Gruyère cheese per person. Cut into slices not more than 2½ cm (1 in) thick, and flour, egg and breadcrumb them. Deep-fry in hot fat or oil until golden brown. Serve hot within 20 minutes.

Savoury Soufflés and Puddings

VEGETABLE SOUFFLÉ

GEMÜSEAUFLAUF

120 g (4 oz) each:
diced carrots
runner beans, sliced small
very small brussels sprouts
mushrooms, sliced
peas

90 g (3 oz) butter
60 g (2 oz) flour
1 dl (4 oz) milk
salt, pepper
4 eggs, separated

Boil the carrots, beans, peas and sprouts in 2½ dl (½ pint) of slightly salted water. If only large sprouts are available, halve or quarter them. Drain. Cook the mushrooms in 30 g (1 oz) butter. Make a white sauce from 60 g (2 oz) butter, flour and milk. Allow to cool a little before stirring in the egg yolks. Stir in all the vegetables, and season to taste. Lastly fold in the stiffly beaten whites of egg. Transfer the mixture to a greased and floured soufflé dish, and bake at 200° C (400° F) for 40 minutes, or until the top is firm and lightly browned. Serve at once with a Cheese Sauce (p. 101).

VEGETABLE PUDDING GEMÜSEDUNSTKOCH

Follow the recipe for Vegetable Soufflé (p. 40), but transfer the mixture to a greased and floured pudding basin, secure the top, and steam for 40 minutes. Turn out and serve with a Cheese Sauce (p. 101).

BEETROOT SOUFFLÉ ROTER RÜBEN AUFLAUF

Boil 480g (1 lb) beetroot in their skins until tender. Peel, and pass through a sieve or a blender. Follow the recipe for Vegetable Soufflé (p. 40) using the beetroot purée instead of any other vegetable, and bake for 40 minutes at 200°–220°C (400°–420°F).

A purée made from 480 g (1 lb) spinach in the same basic recipe makes SPINACH SOUFFLÉ

HAM SOUFFLÉ SCHINKENAUFLAUF

480 g (1 lb) boiled ham, or lean gammon
30 g (1 oz) butter
60 g (2 oz) flour
1 dl (4 oz) milk
salt, pepper, grated nutmeg
4 eggs, separated

Mince the boiled ham or chop very small. Make a white sauce from the butter, flour and milk, add seasonings to taste, and stir in the lightly beaten egg yolks and the minced ham. Finally fold in the stiffly beaten whites of egg. Transfer to a greased and floured soufflé dish and bake in a moderate oven for about 1 hour, until the mixture has set. As this is not a true soufflé, it can be kept hot for a while before serving.

LIVER PUDDING LEBERDUNSTKOCH

480 g (1 lb) liver
60 g (2 oz) stale white bread
120 g (4 oz) butter or margarine
3 eggs, separated
1 dl (4 oz) sour cream
60 g (2 oz) homemade breadcrumbs
salt, pepper

Scrape the liver with a blunt knife and discard all skins. Soak the bread in water, and squeeze out thoroughly. Pass the liver and bread through a sieve, or mince very finely, or put in an electric blender. Cream the margarine with the egg yolks and stir in the liver purée, sour cream, breadcrumbs and salt and pepper to taste. Fold in the stiffly beaten whites of egg. Transfer the mixture to a large, greased and floured pudding basin, cover the top securely and steam for 1 hour. Turn out and serve, as soon as possible, with a salad.

MUSHROOM SOUFFLÉ SCHWAMMERLAUFLAUF

240 g (8 oz) mushrooms	*1 dl (4 oz) milk*
60 g (2 oz) flour	*salt, pepper*
60 g (2 oz) butter	*3 eggs, separated*

Pour boiling water over the sliced mushrooms, and leave them for a few minutes. Drain. Make a white sauce from the butter, flour and milk, add salt and pepper, and when the sauce has cooled down a little stir in the egg yolks followed by the mushrooms. Fold in the stiffly beaten whites of egg. Transfer the mixture to a greased and floured soufflé dish, and bake in a hot oven, 200°–220° C (400°–420° F), for 40 minutes. Serve at once.

POTATO PUDDING KARTOFFELDUNSTKOCH

480 g (1 lb) potatoes	*about 1 dl (3–4 oz) milk*
90 g (3 oz) butter	*salt, pepper, grated nutmeg*
3 eggs, separated	

Mash the boiled potatoes with the butter. When the purée has cooled a little, stir in the egg yolks lightly beaten with some of the milk. Add the remainder of the milk as needed to make the purée soft but not runny. Add seasonings to taste and lastly fold in the stiffly beaten whites of egg. Transfer the mixture to a greased and floured pudding basin, secure the top and steam for 40 minutes. Turn out and serve as soon as possible. Serve with mushroom sauce, or Cheese Sauce (p. 101).

SPINACH PUDDING
SPINATDUNSTKOCH

*480 g (1 lb) spinach (about 300 g
  (10 oz) frozen)*
3 eggs, separated
90 g (3 oz) butter or margarine

*45 g (1½ oz) homemade
  breadcrumbs*
½ dl (2 oz) sour cream
salt, pepper

Boil the spinach in the minimum of water, drain thoroughly and make into a purée. Cream the butter with the egg yolks, stir in the spinach purée, breadcrumbs, sour cream, salt and pepper and fold in the stiffly beaten whites of egg. Transfer the mixture to a greased and floured pudding basin, secure the top and steam for 40 minutes. Turn out and serve as soon as possible. The pudding can be served with scrambled eggs arranged round the bottom.

Fish

Sadly, my original recipes, for fresh-water fish and for crayfish caught in the Austrian lakes, rivers and mountain streams, do not travel well to Britain. I have, however, adapted some to be used with sea fish.

CARP IN ASPIC

GESULZTER KARPFEN

1 kg (2 lb) carp
90 g (3 oz) each:
  parsnip
  carrots
  celery

90 g (3 oz) onion
salt, peppercorns, pickling spice,
  vinegar

Cut the de-scaled and cleaned carp into thick slices. Bring 1 l (2 pints) of salted water to the boil with the peppercorns, the pickling spice, vinegar, and the roughly chopped vegetables. Simmer for 5 minutes, add the carp, and boil gently for 20 minutes. Separate the fish and put it in a dish large enough to hold both it and the stock. Strain the stock into a bowl and discard vegetables. When the stock has cooled a little pour it over the fish and allow it to jelly. Keep in the refrigerator for several hours before serving.

BAKED CARP

GEBRATENER KARPFEN

1 kg (2 lb) carp, in one piece
salt

120 g (4 oz) fat
150 g (5 oz) butter

Rub the scaled and cleaned carp with salt and transfer it to a baking tin in which the fat has been heated. Bake in a moderately hot oven, basting frequently with the juices in the pan. Serve the fish in the skimmed gravy. Melt the butter till nut-brown and pour over the fish.

CARP may also be cut into 1½ in-thick pieces, and fried in egg and breadcrumbs.

FISH GOULASH   FISCHGULASCH

1 kg (2 lb) cod fillets   *1 dessertspoon vinegar*
60 g (2 oz) flour   *1 tablespoon paprika*
salt   *1 dl (4 oz) sour cream*
120 g (4 oz) fat   *60 g (2 oz) tomato purée*
60 g (2 oz) diced fat bacon   *5½ dl (1 pint) beef stock*
240 g (8 oz) chopped onion   *salt, pepper*

Cut the fish into pieces as for a stew and dredge with the sifted salt and flour. Gently fry the bacon in the fat, add the fish and cook. Remove and keep hot. Soften the onion in the juices and fat in the pan, add the vinegar, paprika, sour cream, tomato purée, seasonings and about 6 dl (1 pint) beef stock. Bring to the boil and simmer and stir for a few minutes. Transfer the fish to the sauce and simmer a little longer before serving.

FISH DUMPLINGS   FISCHNOCKERLN

480 g (1 lb) white fish   *2 eggs*
180 g (6 oz) stale white bread   *180 g (6 oz) butter*
*   soaked in milk, squeezed out*   *chopped parsley*
1 dl (4 oz) single cream   *salt, pepper, flour*

Shred the steamed fish taking care to pick out all bones. Stir into a smooth paste with the bread, single cream, eggs, melted butter, parsley, salt and pepper. Let the mixture rest in a cool place for about ½ hour. Scoop out portions with a tablespoon, roll into dumpling shape, dredge with a little flour and poach in nearly boiling water— the water should 'tremble'—for 10 minutes. Drain carefully and serve at once.

FRESH HADDOCK or COD FILLETS IN SOUR CREAM SAUCE
WEISSER FISCH IN RAHMSOSS

1 kg (2 lb) fish fillets
120 g (4 oz) butter or margarine

1 dl (4 oz) sour cream
salt pepper.

Fry the fish gently in the butter, then keep hot while you make the sauce. Stir sour cream, salt and pepper into the fish juices, bring to the boil and pour over the fish in the serving dish.

For HADDOCK or COD FILLETS IN ANCHOVY SAUCE (IN SARDEL-LENSOSS), instead of sour cream, stir sieved anchovy fillets, or anchovy concentrate, into the sauce.

HADDOCK or COD FILLETS WITH SAUCE VINAIGRETTE
WEISSER FISCH MIT SAURER SOSS

Fry the fish gently in butter or margarine, then keep hot while you make the sauce. Stir into the juices in the pan:

1 tablespoon wine vinegar
3 tablespoons salad oil
1 dessertspoon finely chopped fresh herbs

1 dessertspoon gherkins, diced small
salt, pepper

Bring nearly to the boil and pour over the fish in the serving dish.

HERRINGS or MACKERELS WITH SOUR CREAM
HERINGE ODER MAKRELEN MIT RAHM

Grill or fry the filleted fish in your usual way, then stir sour cream into the juices in the pan. Pour over the fish.

ROLLMOPS

6 herrings
240 g (8 oz) finely chopped onion
about 2¼ dl (½ pint) water
about 2¼ dl (½ pint) vinegar

60 g (2 oz) pickling spice
3 bay leaves
salt
1 dessertspoon sugar

Cut off the fish heads and tails, clean and fillet. Put some of the onion on each fillet and roll up tight. Secure with wooden tooth-picks. Bring the water to the boil with vinegar, sugar, pickling spice, bay leaves and salt. Pack the rolled fillets tightly in an oven-proof dish, and pour the hot spiced liquid over. Put in a moderately hot oven for about 15 minutes, when the fish should be cooked. Sprinkle the remaining onion over the fish and serve cold.

FISH AU GRATIN ON SPINACH

GRATINIERTER FISCH AUF SPINAT

1 *kg* (*2 lb*) *sole* or *plaice* or *fresh
    haddock fillets*
fish bones and heads, if possible
*a good handful each of onion and
    parsley, finely chopped*
salt
480 g (*1 lb*) *spinach* (*about 300 g*
    (*10 oz*) *frozen*)
120 g (*4 oz*) *butter or margarine*
240 g (*8 oz*) *potato, boiled and
    peeled*

For the white sauce:
90 g (*3 oz*) *butter or margarine*
45 g (*1½ oz*) *flour*
60 g (*2 oz*) *grated Parmesan or
    other cheese*
1 egg
fish stock and milk as needed
salt, pepper
15 g (*½ oz*) *homemade
    breadcrumbs*

Boil the fish bones and heads with the onion and parsley in a little salted water to make strong stock. Strain the stock into a bowl. Steam the fish quickly in some of the stock. Keep the fish hot while you purée the hot potatoes with 60 g (2 oz) butter, pepper and salt. Keep hot. Cook the spinach, drain thoroughly, chop roughly, and stir in the remainder of the butter. Grease an ovenproof dish, large and deep enough to hold all the ingredients. Put the spinach at the bottom, place the fish over it and pipe or spoon a thick wreath of potato purée round the edge of the dish. Keep hot while you make a thick white sauce from the butter, flour, cheese and fish stock and milk. Add salt and pepper to taste. When it has cooled down a little, stir in the lightly beaten egg. Fill up the free centre space with the sauce (do not cover the potato), sprinkle with breadcrumbs and flakes of butter and put in a hot oven for 10 to 15 minutes until the sauce is bubbling and nicely browned. To make things easier you can make the potato purée earlier, and heat it up when it is needed by stirring in hot milk in which the butter has been melted.

SOLE WITH MUSHROOM SAUCE
GEBRATENE SEEZUNGE MIT SCHWAMMERLSOSS

1 kg (2 lb) sole or *plaice fillets,* *and the bones and heads*	*60 g (2 oz) butter*
salt, pepper	*1 dl (4 oz) double cream*
120 g (4 oz) sliced mushrooms	*dash of lemon juice*

Boil the fish bones and heads in some salted water to make strong stock. Strain into a bowl. Steam the fish fillets in some of the stock, to which a little pepper is added. Remove carefully and keep hot. Boil the fish stock fast to reduce to 2½ dl (½ pint). Cook the mushrooms in the butter and stir into the fish stock together with the double cream. Add a dash of lemon and salt and pepper to taste. Stir and *just* bring to the boil. Transfer the fish fillets to a fireproof dish, pour the sauce over and put under a hot grill until the top is browned. Serve at once.

BLUE TROUT
BLAUGEKOCHTE FORELLEN

one 180–240 g (6–9 oz) trout per person

This dish can only be made from lake or river trout killed no more than 1 hour before cooking. Do *not* cut off the heads and *do not fillet*, but slit the body and gut the fish. Touch the outside of the fish as little as possible to protect the jelly which covers the skin and gives it the blue colour when cooked. Use a fish kettle or a large pan to bring water to the boil, to which salt, some peppercorns and a little vinegar have been added. Immerse the fish carefully, lower the temperature and simmer until the eyes pop out and look like little white balls. Carefully transfer the fish to a serving dish, long enough to take the fish full length, and decorate with sprigs of parsley. Serve melted butter in a separate dish. Blue trout can be served cold with homemade mayonnaise.

Vegetables and Salads

In Viennese homes and good restaurants, vegetables are cooked in the smallest possible amount of salted boiling water, and before serving melted butter or margarine is added, or the vegetable is coated with a white sauce made from the vegetable stock. A popular garnish for many vegetables is a liberal sprinkling of homemade breadcrumbs lightly fried in butter. Salads are, of course, always served with a dressing.

Vegetables

GLOBE ARTICHOKES   ARTISCHOKEN

1 artichoke per person

Throw away the stems and the first round of leaves. Cut off the sharp hard points of the leaves. Wash the artichokes thoroughly under the cold tap. Immerse them in salted boiling water for about 40 minutes—they are cooked when a leaf can be pulled out easily. Drain. Serve melted butter in a separate dish with hot artichokes, and homemade mayonnaise with cold ones.

JERUSALEM ARTICHOKES   TOPINAMBUR

Jerusalem artichokes are difficult to peel because of all their protuberances. I scrub them first with a stiff plastic vegetable brush. If the vegetable is not too dried up this will get some of the skin off and make peeling a little easier. Cut the peeled artichokes into pieces of about equal size and immediately (to prevent their discolouring) boil in salted water until tender. Strain into a bowl—the stock is particularly useful for adding to soups or gravies. Transfer to a serving dish and sprinkle liberally with homemade breadcrumbs fried in butter or margarine.

SALSIFY is a near relative (though easier to clean) and is cooked the same way.

AUBERGINES   EIERÖLFRÜCHTE

Cut off the stems of the aubergines and if the skin is at all tough, peel them. Halve, and remove the pips, then cut into lengths or rounds. Fry finely chopped onion and crushed garlic in oil over a low heat. Add the aubergines and salt and pepper. Cover the pan and cook gently until the aubergines are tender. They can also be casseroled in the oven.

HARICOT BEANS   WEISSE BOHNEN

Soak the beans overnight in cold water. Put into fresh cold salted water and boil until tender. (This will take at least an hour.) Drain into a bowl. Make a roux from some fat, in which you have softened some finely chopped onion, and flour, salt and pepper. Pour on enough of the bean stock to make a thick sauce. Add more salt and pepper and a little vinegar, to taste. Return the beans to the sauce and simmer for a few minutes.

RED CABBAGE   ROTKRAUT

1 red cabbage, about 720 g (1½ lb)   *salt, pepper, caraway seeds*
60 g (2 oz) shredded onion   *2½ dl (½ pint) cheap red wine, or*
120 g (4 oz) fat or dripping   *wine vinegar/sugar/water*
1 dessertspoon flour   *substitute*
30 g (1 oz) sugar

Soften the shredded cabbage and onion in the fat. Continuing over a low heat, stir in the sugar, salt, pepper, caraway seeds and flour.

Cook and stir for a few moments. Pour on the wine, or substitute, and enough beef or vegetable stock just to cover the cabbage. Simmer in the covered pan until the cabbage is tender. Add a little boiling water if needed but keep the liquid to a minimum. Red cabbage improves on re-heating.

WHITE CABBAGE, BRAISED (GEDÜNSTETES KRAUT) is prepared and cooked the same way, but use beef or vegetable stock instead of the wine and 1 tablespoon vinegar.

CARROTS   KAROTTEN

Dice or slice the carrots. Melt some butter or margarine—60 g (2 oz) to 480 g (1 lb) carrots—with one dessertspoon of sugar and glaze the carrots in a covered saucepan. Add salt and pepper, dust with a little flour, and stir for a few moments. Add cold water to cover the carrots, and bring to the boil while stirring to dissolve all lumps. Cook in the covered pan until the carrots are tender.

CELERIAC   ZELLER

Allow 120–180 g (4–6 oz) fat or oil to 1 root of celeriac, about 720 g (1½ lb). Peel the celeriac, cut into quarters or eighths, according to the size of the vegetable, and cut into rounds ½ cm (¼ in) thick. Fry gently in the fat or oil, adding a little salt and pepper, until the vegetable is golden brown.

KOHLRABI

Kohlrabi is a root vegetable that grows into a turnip-like globe. (They are easy to grow.)

Allow 1 medium-sized kohlrabi per person. Peel, cut into halves and slice about ½ cm (¼ in) thick. Boil in slightly salted water until tender. Strain, and make a thick parsley sauce with the stock. Transfer the kohlrabi to the sauce and simmer for a few moments. If the globes are very young the tuft of leaves on top can be chopped and cooked with the vegetable. Kohlrabi may also be simply boiled and served sprinkled with lightly fried breadcrumbs.

LENTILS

SÜSS–SAURE LINSEN

Use the large, continental lentils.

480 g (1 lb) lentils	*30 g (1 oz) sugar*
120 g (4 oz) fat or dripping	*60 g (2 oz) flour*
finely chopped onion	*salt, pepper*
finely chopped parsley	*1 tablespoon vinegar*

Spread the lentils on a tray and pick out any pieces of wood or grit. Wash in a sieve under the cold tap. (The cooking time will be halved if you soak overnight.) Transfer to a saucepan of cold water, bring to the boil and cook until the lentils are tender—30–40 minutes, if unsoaked. Strain, and reserve the stock. Soften the onion and parsley in the fat, dust with flour and continue stirring over a low heat. Add sugar, salt and pepper, vinegar and about 1½ dl (¼ pint) of the lentil stock. Bring to the boil stirring, and continue until the sauce is smooth and thick. Add the lentils and simmer for a few minutes. There should be just enough liquid left to keep the lentils moist. This dish improves on re-heating. Lentils go particularly well with any sort of boiled sausage and with boiled ham or gammon.

COS LETTUCE

KOCHSALAT

Cut 1 or 2 large cos lettuces into thick slices. Boil quickly in salted water. Strain and reserve the stock. Fry a clove of crushed garlic in margarine, and make a sauce with flour and the stock. Season. Chop the lettuce and transfer to the sauce. Simmer for a few minutes.

Peas, up to half the weight of the lettuce, can be cooked with the lettuce, making BRAISED LETTUCE AND PEAS (KOCHSALAT UND ERBSEN).

VEGETABLE MARROW

KÜRBIS

1 or 2 vegetable marrows, about	*finely chopped parsley*
1 kg (2 lb)	*120 g (4 oz) butter or margarine*
salt	*chopped dill, optional*
120 g (4 oz) finely sliced onion	*1 dessertspoon paprika*

45 g (1½ oz) flour
about 2½ dl (½ pint) vegetable
stock or water

1 dl (4 oz) sour cream
120 g (4 oz) tomato purée
1 dessertspoon vinegar

Halve the peeled marrow and remove the pips. Cut the marrow into thin strips about 5 cm (2 in) long. Cover with salt and leave for about 40 minutes. Meanwhile soften the onion, parsley and dill in the butter, add the paprika and flour and stir over a low heat for a few moments. Add about 2½ dl (½ pint) vegetable stock or water to make a smooth sauce. Stir in the tomato purée, sour cream and bring to the boil again while stirring. Rinse the salted marrow under the cold tap before folding it lightly into the sauce. Cover the pan and simmer for about 15 minutes. Add a little water or stock if needed, but keep the liquid to a minimum. Add salt if necessary.

For VEGETABLE MARROW WITH BREADCRUMBS (KÜRBIS AUF POLNISCHE ART) prepare the marrow as in the above recipe. Boil the strips in lightly salted water until soft. Drain. Transfer to a serving dish and cover the vegetable with homemade breadcrumbs fried in butter or margarine.

SAUERKRAUT

I used to make sauerkraut in the past, but it is a lot of work which goes on for weeks and since it is now easily available in this country, I shall not give the recipe. Whether you buy the sauerkraut open from a barrel or in a jar, it is cooked the same way: simply empty the sauerkraut into a saucepan, add a little boiling water and cook over medium heat until it is soft and heated through. Stir in a knob of butter or margarine and some caraway seeds. Sauerkraut can be re-heated.

SPINACH PURÉE   SPINAT AUF WIENER ART

720 g (1½ lb) spinach
90 g (3 oz) butter or margarine
45 g (1½ oz) flour

1 section crushed garlic
salt, pepper

Wash the spinach very thoroughly. Drain. Boil in *very* little salted water. Strain carefully and reserve the stock. Sieve the spinach, or blend in a liquidizer. Fry the garlic lightly in the butter, dust with flour, add salt and pepper and cook for a few moments over a low heat. Pour on about 3 dl (½ pint) of the spinach stock. Stir and boil for a few moments. Fold in the spinach purée and simmer for a minute.

Vegetable Dishes

STUFFED CABBAGE LEAVES KOHLWÜRSTEL

10 or 12 large leaves from a
  Savoy cabbage
480 g (1 lb) minced meat
90 g (3 oz) finely chopped onion
chopped parsley

60 g (2 oz) fat or dripping
1 egg
salt, pepper, marjoram
120 g (4 oz) fat bacon
1½ dl (¼ pint) beef bouillon
1 dl (4 oz) sour cream

Boil the cabbage leaves in slightly salted water until they are pliable but not cooked—about 3 to 5 minutes. Drain carefully and leave on one side while you make the stuffing. Soften about two-thirds of your chopped onion with the parsley in the fat and stir them into the minced meat together with the egg, salt, pepper and marjoram. Lay out a leaf, flat, and half-cover it with stuffing. Roll up the leaf tightly and place in an ovenproof casserole which has been lined with rashers of bacon. Pack the casserole tightly with stuffed leaves. Sprinkle the remaining chopped onion over the top (and any mince that is left over) and pour on the bouillon. Bake in a hot oven for about 40 minutes, when the cabbage should have changed colour and be very tender. Stir the sour cream into the gravy and return to the oven for another 5 minutes.

CAULIFLOWER AND HAM GEFÜLLTER KARFIOL

1 large cauliflower
120 g (4 oz) butter or margarine
2 eggs

180 g (6 oz) boiled ham or
  gammon, chopped small
1 dl (4 oz) sour cream

120 g (4 oz) grated Parmesan,   salt, pepper
  Emmental, Gruyère or
  Cheddar cheese

Cut the stem of the cauliflower close, and keep only the most tender inside leaves. Boil in salted water until tender. Meanwhile make the sauce: cream the butter with two egg yolks, stir in the chopped meat, grated cheese, sour cream and salt and pepper. Lastly fold in two stiffly beaten whites of egg. Transfer the cooked and drained cauliflower to a greased and floured soufflé dish. Pour or spoon the sauce evenly over the cauliflower and put in a moderately hot oven for about 30 minutes. Serve at once.

VEGETABLE FRITTERS   GEMÜSE IN BACKTEIG

Cauliflower, salsify, celeriac and medium-sized, firm mushrooms are the most suitable vegetables to be fried in batter. Divide the cauliflower into sprigs, slice the peeled and quartered celeriac 1 cm ($\frac{1}{2}$ in) thick, cut the salsify into $2\frac{1}{2}$ cm (1 in) lengths. They should all be parboiled and drained before being coated in thick batter and fried golden brown in fat or oil. Use the caps of mushrooms and coat in batter without any previous cooking. Serve as soon as possible. A mixture of several of the vegetables makes a very good dish.

MUSHROOMS IN BREADCRUMBS

CHAMPIGNON GEBACKEN

Use only the caps of medium-sized, firm mushrooms. Dredge with flour, dip into egg lightly beaten with a little salt, and coat with homemade breadcrumbs. Deep-fry in hot fat or oil until golden brown. Serve hot with a salad or with Tartare sauce.

HOT STUFFED TOMATOES   GEFÜLLTE PARADEIS, HEISS

10 fairly large tomatoes   60 g (2 oz) sliced mushrooms
240 g (8 oz) minced meat   chopped parsley
60 g (2 oz) finely chopped onion 60 g (2 oz) butter or fat

1 egg
salt, pepper
30 g (1 oz) grated Parmesan or
  other cheese

30 g (1 oz) homemade
  breadcrumbs

Gently fry the onion, parsley and mushrooms in the fat, push to one side and, continuing over a low heat, brown the meat all over. Transfer to a mixing bowl and add the lightly beaten egg; season. Cut a slice off the top of each tomato and scoop out the flesh taking care not to pierce the skin. Fill the tomato shells with the meat mixture—into which some or all of the puréed tomato flesh can be stirred—and place the tomatoes in a greased ovenproof dish, large enough to hold them in one layer. Sprinkle the tomatoes with grated cheese and breadcrumbs, dot with butter and put in a hot oven for about 10 minutes.

Salads

I dress almost any left-over cooked vegetable as a salad—runner beans, celery, celeriac, leeks, salsify and cauliflower. All these, and potato salad, are improved by being tossed in an oil and vinegar dressing several hours in advance or overnight. Lettuce and other green salad should be dressed at the last moment.

MIXED SALAD   GEMISCHTER SALAT

Any variety of vegetables can be used in this salad. I like it best made from peppers, tomatoes, white cabbage, cucumbers and a little cooked beetroot. Cut the tops off the peppers, empty them of pips and cut into thin rings. Cut the tomatoes into quarters. Slice the peeled cucumber thinly. (If the cucumber is very young it need not be peeled.) Dice the beetroot, but don't use too much, for its taste and colour will swamp everything else. Shred the cabbage. Make a dressing of 1 part vinegar, 2 parts oil, salt and pepper, to which shredded onion can be added. Pour this over the vegetables in a salad bowl, and toss. Stoned olives can be added, as well as sliced or quartered hard-boiled eggs.

BEETROOT SALAD ROTER RÜBENSALAT

Boil beetroot until tender. Peel and dice, or slice. Make a dressing from 1 part vinegar, 2 parts oil, salt, pepper, French mustard, grated fresh horseradish (if not available, use dried) and a little sugar. Pour over the hot beetroot and toss. Serve cold.

CARROT SALAD KAROTTENSALAT

Stir into the grated carrots a dressing made from 1 part vinegar, 3 parts oil, salt, pepper and sugar. Let the salad stand for at least 1 hour before serving.

CELERIAC SALAD ZELLERSALAT

Peel the celeriac, and cut it in half or quarters, according to size. Cut into slices about 5 mm ($\frac{1}{4}$ in) thick, and boil in slightly salted water, to which a dash of lemon juice has been added, until tender. Drain, and while still hot, toss in a dressing made from 1 part vinegar, 2 parts oil, salt, pepper and a pinch of sugar. Serve hot or cold.

COLESLAW KRAUTSALAT

Shred the cabbage finely into a bowl. Scald with boiling water and leave the cabbage immersed for about 5 minutes. Drain. Toss the cabbage, while still hot, in a dressing made from 1 part vinegar, 2 parts oil, salt, pepper, French mustard and caraway seeds. If liked, add some finely chopped onion. Serve hot with hot sausages or hot boiled ham: serve cold with cold meat. Instead of a vinegar and oil dressing, homemade mayonnaise can be used for the cold cabbage.

LENTIL SALAD   LINSENSALAT

Cook the lentils according to the recipe in the section on Vegetables. Make a dressing of 1 part vinegar, 2 parts oil, finely chopped onion, salt, pepper and a little sugar. Pour the dressing over the drained hot lentils and serve cold.

HARICOT BEAN SALAD (BOHNENSALAT) is prepared the same way, but omit the sugar in the dressing.

MEAT SALAD   FLEISCHSALAT

Brawn, extrawurst, garlic sausage, cold roast pork or beef can all be used for this salad, either singly or mixed. Slice some onion finely, chop some parsley and cut the meat into neat dice. Toss all ingredients in a dressing made of 1 part vinegar, 2 parts oil, French mustard, crushed garlic, salt and pepper. The salad can be decorated with quartered hard-boiled eggs.

MUSHROOM SALAD   SCHWAMMERLSALAT

Use fresh button mushrooms, or slightly bigger ones provided the underside of the mushrooms is still pink and the edge curled in. If the mushrooms have earth on them, wash them in cold water under the tap, otherwise it should be enough to rub them with salt in a basin. Rinse under the cold tap. Tiny button mushrooms can be left whole, bigger ones should be cut to a suitable size before tossing in a dressing made from 1 part vinegar, 2 or 3 parts oil, and salt and pepper. Let the salad stand for an hour or two before serving.

POTATO SALAD   KARTOFFELSALAT

240 g (8 oz) potatoes　　　　　　*pepper*
60 g (2 oz) beef bouillon or stock　*French mustard*
Dressing:　　　　　　　　　　　*finely chopped onion to taste*
2 tablespoons vinegar　　　　　*4 tablespoons oil*
salt

Boil the potatoes in their skins. Peel, and dice or slice. While the potatoes are still hot pour on the bouillon and the dressing. Potato salad improves by being made the previous day.

RUSSIAN SALAD

*120 g (4 oz) boiled, peeled
  potatoes*
120 g (4 oz) apples
60 g (2 oz) pickled gherkins
60 g (2 oz) chopped onion
2 tinned anchovy fillets

60 g (2 oz) cooked peas
2 hard-boiled eggs
*1 dl (4 oz) homemade
  mayonnaise*
parsley

Dice the peeled and cored apples and the gherkins, chop the anchovy fillets and stir together lightly with the diced potatoes, onion and peas. Fold in most of the mayonnaise. Decorate with whole or halved hard-boiled eggs, coated with a little mayonnaise and sprinkled with parsley.

SAUSAGE SALAD

3 pairs frankfurter sausages
*120 g (4 oz) Gruyère or
  Emmental cheese*
480 g (1 lb) grated white cabbage
Dressing:
1 clove garlic, crushed

2 tablespoons (2 oz) vinegar
4 tablespoons (4 oz) oil
*1 tablespoon (1 oz) strong, hot
  beef bouillon*
salt, pepper

Immerse the frankfurter sausages in boiling water, turn off the heat and leave them in the water for about 5 minutes. Drain, and cut into 1 cm ($\frac{1}{2}$ in) slices. Cut the cheese into 1 cm ($\frac{1}{2}$ in) dice. Pour boiling water over the finely shredded or grated cabbage and leave immersed for about 5 minutes. Drain, and while the cabbage is still hot, pour on the dressing. Toss, and allow it to get cold before adding the sausage and cheese. Toss vigorously and serve cold.

COLD STUFFED TOMATOES

Allow a whole or half tomato per person, depending on size. Cut a slice off the top of each tomato, and scoop out the flesh taking care not to pierce the skin. Dice peeled and cored apples, and inner celery stalks, and coat with homemade mayonnaise. Stir in the sieved tomato flesh, and fill the tomatoes. Keep in the refrigerator for at least 1 hour before serving.

Dumplings,
Potatoes and Cereals

There are two kinds of dumplings in Viennese cookery, '*Knödel*' and '*Nockerln*', for which there is only one word—dumpling—in English. There is, however, quite a difference between the two. *Knödel* are round in shape, rolled between the palms of the hands, and they usually contain more eggs than *Nockerln*. These are scooped out with a spoon from the mixture, and shaped like plums. Both kinds of dumplings are served as garnishes for soups—you will find other recipes for them in the section on soups—and they go very well with stews of all kinds. They are sometimes served as a course on their own with a salad or with scrambled eggs. When using recipes from the section on Soups, double or treble the quantities, and make bigger dumplings.

Dumplings

BREAD DUMPLINGS   SEMMELKNÖDEL

Makes 8–10 dumplings

240 g (8 oz) crusty white bread
    or bread rolls, diced
finely chopped onion
finely chopped parsley
90 g (3 oz) fat or dripping

about 1 dl (3–4 oz) milk
2 eggs
60–90 g (2–3 oz) flour
salt, pepper

Fry the diced bread, the onion and parsley in the fat until the bread is golden brown and crisp. Put into a bowl. Whisk the milk, eggs, salt and pepper and pour over the fried bread. Stand for about 15 minutes to allow the bread to absorb the liquid. Pour off any surplus. Fold in enough flour to make a workable dough. Lightly roll portions of the mixture between your floured palms into dumplings of about 5 cm (2 in) diameter. Lower into lightly boiling salted water and cook gently but steadily for about 10 minutes. Drain. Serve with boiled ham, with sweet and sour lights, or with stews or braised meat. Any left-over dumplings can be sliced and fried in fat until crisp. Serve these with scrambled eggs or with a salad.

HAM DUMPLINGS   SCHINKENKNÖDEL

Follow the recipe for bread dumplings and add 150 g (5 oz) cooked diced ham or gammon to the mixture. Form dumplings of about 7½ cm (3 in) diameter, lower into lightly boiling salted water and boil for 15 minutes. Serve as a light meal with a salad. The dumplings are bigger, and will therefore be fewer.

BREADCRUMB DUMPLINGS   BRÖSELKNÖDEL

60 g (2 oz) stale white bread, soaked in water
60 g (2 oz) butter or margarine
finely chopped parsley
10 g (¼ oz) fat

60 g (2 oz) homemade breadcrumbs
1 egg
salt, pepper

Cream the butter with the soaked and squeezed-out bread. Stir in the parsley, softened in fat, the egg, breadcrumbs, salt and pepper. With two teaspoons form small dumplings, immerse into lightly boiling salted water and simmer for about 10 minutes. Drain. Add the dumplings as a garnish to soups, or to chicken or veal in, say, a white sauce.

PARMESAN CHEESE DUMPLINGS   PARMESANKNÖDEL

120 g (4 oz) butter or margarine
2 eggs, separated
1 heaped tablespoon homemade breadcrumbs

180 g (6 oz) grated Parmesan cheese
salt, pepper

Cream the butter with the yolks of egg. Stir in the grated cheese, breadcrumbs, salt and pepper. The mixture should have a workable consistency—if it is too soft stir in more breadcrumbs. Fold in the stiffly beaten whites of egg. Scoop out portions with a tablespoon, lower carefully into lightly boiling salted water. Simmer for 10 minutes. Lift out the dumplings with a perforated spoon and transfer to a serving dish. Serve with a stew or with braised meat. The dumplings make an excellent course served on their own accompanied by a Cheese Sauce (p. 101) and salad.

FLOUR DUMPLINGS   MEHLNOCKERLN

240 g (8 oz) self-raising flour
1 egg
1 dl (1 gill) milk

salt
90 g (3 oz) butter

Stir egg, milk, flour and salt into the creamed butter. Stir until the mixture leaves the spoon. Scoop out dumplings with a dessertspoon, lower carefully into lightly boiling salted water. Simmer for about 10 minutes. Drain into a large sieve and douse for a second or two under the cold tap. This prevents the dumplings from sticking together. Serve with a stew, or serve the dumplings tossed in melted butter and accompanied by a salad.

EGG DUMPLINGS   EIERNOCKERLN

Make Flour Dumplings (above), then transfer the dumplings to a frying-pan in which margarine has been melted. Beat 2 eggs with sour milk or sour cream or yoghurt, and salt and pepper, and pour over the dumplings in the pan. Cook gently until the mixture has set. Serve at once with a green salad.

MEAT DUMPLINGS   FLEISCHNOCKERLN

150 g (5 oz) margarine   *1 egg*
60 g (2 oz) flour   *240 g (8 oz) minced meat*
1 dl (4 oz) milk   *salt, pepper, marjoram*

Make a white sauce from 30 g (1 oz) margarine, the flour and milk. Cream 120 g (4 oz) margarine until very light and stir in the slightly cooled white sauce. Stir in the beaten egg, minced meat and seasonings to taste. Scoop out portions with a dessertspoon, lower them carefully into lightly boiling salted water. Simmer in the water, which should be 'trembling', for 5 to 10 minutes. Lift out carefully with a sieve or a perforated spoon. Transfer to a serving dish and serve with a salad.

POTATO DUMPLINGS   ERDÄPFELKNÖDEL

240 g (8 oz) potatoes   *30 g (1 oz) flour*
30 g (1 oz) butter or margarine *60 g (2 oz) homemade (dried)*
salt   *breadcrumbs, fried crisp in 90 g*
2 eggs   *(3 oz) butter*

Boil the potatoes in their skins. Peel, and mash with the butter, eggs, flour and salt. Scoop out heaped tablespoons of the mixture and roll lightly between the floured palms of your hands into round dumplings of about 5 cm (2 in) diameter. Immerse carefully into boiling salted water and simmer steadily for about 10 minutes. Lift out with a strainer or a perforated spoon, and serve the dumplings dredged with the crisp breadcrumbs.

LIVER DUMPLINGS   LEBERKNÖDEL

Follow the recipe in the section for soup garnishes. Scoop out portions with a tablespoon and boil in salted water for 10 minutes. Drain and serve with a salad.

POLENTA DUMPLINGS   POLENTANOCKERLN

Follow the recipe for boiled polenta in the cereal section. With a dessertspoon scoop out portions and pile on a serving dish. Sprinkle generously with grated Parmesan cheese, pour on slightly browned melted butter and serve at once with a salad.

SEMOLINA DUMPLINGS   GRIESSNOCKERLN

Follow the recipe in the section for beef broth garnishes. Scoop out portions with a tablespoon and boil in salted water for about 10 minutes. Drain, and serve with a salad.

Potato Dishes

STUFFED BAKED POTATOES   GEFÜLLTE KARTOFFEL

Makes filling for 5–6 potatoes.

*1 potato, weight 150–180 g
  (5–6 oz), per person
60 g (2 oz) butter or margarine
120 g (4 oz) boiled ham or
  gammon, chopped very small*

*1 egg
1–2 tablespoons sour cream
salt, pepper
30 g (1 oz) melted butter*

Bake well-scrubbed potatoes in a roasting dish in a hot to very hot oven for 30 to 40 minutes. Test by gently squeezing. Halve them lengthways and scoop out completely, taking care not to pierce the skins. Mash the flesh with the butter, stir in the egg, lightly beaten with a little sour cream, and the chopped meat. Add sufficient sour cream to give the filling the consistency of very thick cream. Add seasoning to taste. Pile the filling into the potato shells, transfer them to an ovenproof dish, sprinkle them with melted butter and put in a hot oven for 5 to 10 minutes.

Instead of sour cream, curd cheese sieved with a little top of the milk can be used, or the potato flesh can be mashed with plain

C

yoghurt and butter. Instead of the gammon, garlic sausage or frankfurter sausage can be used, or the potatoes can be filled with their own purée as above and when removed from the oven scrambled eggs piled on top.

CREAMY POTATOES   MILCHKARTOFFEL

480 g (1 lb) potatoes   salt, pepper
about 2½ dl (½ pint) milk   finely chopped parsley
60 g (2 oz) butter or margarine

Peel the potatoes and dice or thinly slice them. Add the butter and seasoning to the milk, and simmer the potatoes in it over a low heat until they are soft. Add a little more milk if needed, but keep it to the minimum. Sprinkle with chopped parsley before serving. Alternatively, the milk and potatoes can be cooked in a greased casserole in the oven.

POTATO ESCALOPES   ERDÄPFELSCHNITZEL

600 g (1¼ lb) potatoes   2 eggs
30 g (1 oz) grated Gruyère,   plain flour
    Emmental or Cheddar cheese   salt, pepper
1 knackwurst or 2 frankfurter   flour, eggs and homemade
    sausages, simmered for 5   breadcrumbs for coating the
    minutes   escalopes

Boil the potatoes, peel and mash. Work into a dough with cheese, eggs, salt and pepper, the cooked diced sausage and enough flour to make a workable dough. Divide into portions and pat into hamburger shape. Flour, egg and breadcrumb the escalopes and fry golden brown in hot fat. The escalopes can be kept hot for up to 20 minutes before serving, but they are at their best soon after frying.

POTATO GOULASH   ERDÄPFELGULASCH

720 g (1¼ lb) potatoes   120 g (4 oz) finely chopped onion
90 g (3 oz) fat or dripping   1 dessertspoon paprika

30 g (1 oz) flour	*1 tablespoon concentrated tomato*
1 dl (4 oz) sour cream	*purée*
2⅓ dl (½ pint) vegetable stock or	*salt*
water	

Peel, dice or slice the boiled potatoes. Keep hot while making the sauce. Gently fry the onion in the fat, and continuing over a low heat, stir in the paprika and flour and cook for a few moments. Pour in the water and bring to the boil while stirring smooth. Stir in the sour cream, the tomato purée and seasoning to taste. Fold in the potatoes, and simmer for a few minutes.

HAM CRESCENTS   SCHINKENKIPFELN AUS ERDÄPFELTEIG

180 g (6 oz) potatoes	*salt*
150 g (5 oz) butter or margarine	*240 g (8 oz) cooked, diced ham or*
150 g (5 oz) flour	*gammon*
2 eggs	

Peel the boiled potatoes and mash with the butter. Work into a dough with the flour and eggs, and season to taste. Let the dough rest ½ hour in a cold place. Roll out into 10 cm (4 in) squares. Place a tablespoon of the meat in the centre of each square, fold into triangles and bend into crescents. Brush over with water and secure the edges with a dampened fork. Transfer the crescents to a greased and floured baking sheet and bake in a moderately hot oven for about 15 minutes, or until the pastry feels firm to the touch and is lightly browned. If you wish, the dampened crescents can be sprinkled with salt and caraway seeds before baking. They are best eaten hot soon after leaving the oven, but they can be eaten cold.

HAM AND POTATOES   KARTOFFELAUFLAUF

480 g (1 lb) potatoes	*1 egg*
2 hard-boiled eggs, sliced	*1 dl (4 oz) sour cream*
240 g (8 oz) boiled, diced ham or	*salt, pepper*
gammon	*homemade breadcrumbs*

Boil the potatoes but do not overcook. Peel, and cut into slices.

Cover the bottom of a greased ovenproof dish with a layer of potato, cover this with a layer of sliced eggs, then a layer of chopped ham. Continue thus, finishing with a layer of potato. Stir together the egg and sour cream, and season, taking the saltiness of the ham into account. Pour this evenly over the potatoes, sprinkle with breadcrumbs and dot with flakes of butter. Put into a hot oven for 10 to 15 minutes, until the top is bubbling and nicely browned.

MARJORAM POTATOES   MAJORANKARTOFFEL

Boil, peel and slice the potatoes. Make a roux from equal quantities fat and flour, add a tablespoon of dried marjoram, salt and pepper, a little vinegar to taste, and enough vegetable stock to give the sauce the consistency of boiled custard. Transfer the potatoes to the sauce, take care not to break them up, and leave them immersed, warm, but off direct heat, for about 30 minutes to absorb the full flavour. Bring to the boil before serving.

TYROLEAN POTATOES   TIROLER GERÖSTEL

60 g (2 oz) fat
60 g (2 oz) chopped onion
480 g (1 lb) minced meat
salt, pepper

beef or vegetable stock or water
1 kg (2 lb) potatoes, boiled and
peeled
90 g (3 oz) fat

Fry the onion in 60 g (2 oz) fat until lightly browned. Add the meat, pepper and salt, and just cover with stock or water. The original recipe uses minced pork, but failing this minced beef will do. Simmer until tender. Sauté the sliced potatoes in the remaining fat. Add salt to taste. Lightly mix meat and potatoes together. Instead of fresh mince, left-over roast meat can be used, sliced small and lightly fried together with the potatoes.

POTATO NOODLES   ERDÄPFELNUDELN

480 g (1 lb) potatoes
30 g (1 oz) butter or margarine

1 egg, lightly beaten with a drop
of milk

120–180 g (4–6 oz) flour
salt

60 g (2 oz) homemade
breadcrumbs, lightly fried

Boil the potatoes, peel and mash. While the potato purée is hot, work it into a dough with the butter, egg, salt, and enough flour to make the dough workable. Roll portions into pointed noodles, about the shape and size of toggle buttons, immerse carefully in slightly salted water and simmer gently until the noodles swim on top. Drain. Douse quickly under the cold tap. Toss the noodles in breadcrumbs lightly fried in fat. Serve with venison and game.

POTATO PUFFS   KARTOFFELPUFFER

480 g (1 lb) potatoes
30 g (1 oz) flour
30 g (1 oz) homemade
  breadcrumbs

2–3 tablespoons milk
salt, pepper

Grate the peeled potatoes into cold water. Drain, wrap in a cloth and squeeze out liquid. Quickly stir in the flour, breadcrumbs, salt and pepper and enough milk to bind the dough. Fry heaped tablespoons of the mixture in hot fat until golden brown. While frying, flatten the puffs a little with a fish slice. Lift them out with the fish slice and let surplus fat drip back. Serve with a salad, or make smaller puffs and serve with roast meat.

POTATOES IN SOUR CREAM SAUCE
EINGEBRANNTE KARTOFFEL

480 g (1 lb) potatoes
finely chopped onion
finely chopped parsley
60 g (2 oz) butter or margarine
60 g (2 oz) flour

salt, pepper, 1 bay leaf, fresh or
  dried herbs as wished
1 dl (4 oz) sour cream
about 2½ dl (½ pint) stock or water

Slice the boiled, then peeled, potatoes about 5 mm (¼ in) thick. Keep the potatoes hot while you make the sauce. Soften a little onion and parsley in the butter, dust with flour, add the seasoning

69

and herbs and cook over a low heat for a few moments. Pour in the stock or water, bring to the boil while stirring until smooth. Stir in the sour cream, then fold the potatoes into the sauce. Bring back to the boil before serving.

BAKED POTATO ROUNDS ROHSCHEIBEN

This is a quick and interesting way of cooking potatoes to accompany a joint. I recommend it particularly for the use of old potatoes.

Scrub the potatoes and prick out all blemishes, but do not peel. Dry the potatoes with a cloth and slice them about 5 mm ($\frac{1}{4}$ in) thick. Lay them out on a wet baking sheet—they must not overlap. Bake in a hot oven until the slices are puffed up. This takes between 30 and 45 minutes. Serve as soon as possible.

POTATO STRAWS STROHKARTOFFELN

Shred the peeled potatoes into cold water. Drain and dry with a cloth. Fry in hot fat or oil until the potatoes are crisp and golden brown. Serve as a change from chips.

Cereals

RICE REIS

This is a foolproof method for cooking rice.

Measure the rice in cups. Fry it gently in fat or dripping until most of the grains are nearly transparent. Add salt and pepper. For every cup of rice pour on two cups of cold water. Cook gently in the tightly covered pan until the water has been absorbed by the rice. This method will keep the grains separate. Patna, or long grain, rice gives the best results.

POLENTA   POLENTA

Polenta is Italian maize flour with the consistency of coarse semolina. It goes very well with stewed or braised beef and gravy.

360 g (12 oz) polenta   *about 2 l (3 pints) salted water*

Stir the polenta into the boiling water. When the water has come to the boil again, lower the heat and continue simmering, stirring frequently, until the polenta forms a thick mass which does not stick either to the pan or to the spoon.

FRIED POLENTA   GERÖSTETE POLENTA

Cook the polenta following the previous recipe. Allow it to get cold, cut into slices about 2½ cm (1 in) thick, and fry in fat or dripping until golden brown and crisp all over. Serve with stews.

TARHONYA

Tarhonya is a Hungarian cereal not easy to get in this country, even in Continental delicatessen shops. Melon-seed shaped pasta is a good substitute.

Follow the recipe for rice or boil the tarhonya in salted water until soft. Drain, and gently fry in fat or margarine.

Main Course Meat Dishes

The Viennese way of roasting meat and poultry is obviously very much the same as the British, and I have therefore included here only those recipes which have some special point of interest in method or ingredients. However, I must mention the Viennese method of making gravy to accompany roast meat. Neither gravy powder nor flour for thickening the gravy is ever used. To make the gravy, lift the meat out of the roasting pan and keep hot. Pour very hot water or vegetable stock into the pan, and over a low heat scrape round with a fork to incorporate all the meat juices sticking to the pan. Pour or spoon off as much of the fat as possible and serve the gravy in a separate sauce boat with the roast meat.

A lot of veal is used in Viennese cookery, but veal is expensive in this country and not always very good, so apart from the cheapest stewing veal, I replace all veal with leg or hand of pork. This may be anathema to some cooks, who of course can use veal in any recipe where I give the alternative of using veal or pork. However, I get excellent results with pork, and even my *Wiener Schnitzel* made from pork escalopes has never yet been found sub-standard.

Of the many different Austrian recipes for roast venison I give only one basic one, because the special cuts of stag and roebuck asked for in these recipes are not easily found in Britain.

My own personal way of roasting is to start in a hot oven in a covered pan, or with the meat wrapped in foil or film, to prevent the oven getting spattered with fat. After about three-quarters of the roasting time I remove the cover and allow the meat to brown at a slightly lower temperature, basting frequently. In the case of game birds I wrap them from the start in fat rashers of bacon. When roasting chicken I place a largish knob of butter on the breast for the last 10 minutes of open roasting. This gives the chicken a nice gloss.

BRAISED BEEF   GEDÜNSTETES RINDFLEISCH

180 g (6 oz) sliced onion
180 g (6 oz) fat or dripping

*1 kg (about 2 lb) blade of beef, in
   one thick piece*
salt, pepper, marjoram

Soften the onion in the fat, push to one side and add the meat. Sprinkle in the salt, pepper and marjoram and fry and turn the meat until it is nicely browned all over. Cook in the oven or in a casserole with just enough water or vegetable stock to keep the meat covered, or boil gently in a covered pan with enough liquid to keep it from boiling dry. When the meat is tender, keep it hot while passing the gravy through a sieve. Return both meat and gravy to the pan, bring to the boil once and serve either in one piece or cut into thick slices, with the gravy poured over the meat or served separately.

For BRAISED BEEF WITH SOUR CREAM stir about 1 dl (4 oz) sour cream into the gravy.

For BRAISED BEEF WITH ANCHOVY SAUCE stir concentrated anchovy paste into the gravy.

For BRAISED BEEF WITH MUSTARD SAUCE stir French mustard into the gravy.

For BRAISED BEEF WITH ONIONS use double the quantity of onions and add more fat as required.

BOILED BEEF   SUPPENFLEISCH

About 8 servings

This is a Viennese speciality, and for real luxury fillet of beef is boiled. However, I use good quality braising beef.

*1½ kg (3 lb) braising beef, cut in
   one thick piece*
beef bones, if available

90 g (3 oz) each:
parsnip
carrots

73

90 g (3 oz) each:
   onion
   celery

3 l (6 pints) water
salt

Crush the bones, chop the vegetables roughly and bring to the boil in the slightly salted water. Add the meat, cover the pan and simmer gently until the meat is tender. Carve at table or arrange slices of the meat in a dish. With the meat serve separately one of the following sauces: Horseradish and Apple, Chives, Dill or Caper. Serve a little of the stock with the meat and use the remainder of the stock for a soup.

BEEF ESCALOPES

RINDSSCHNITZEL

1 kg (2 lb) blade of beef, cut into
   escalopes
180–240 g (6–8 oz) finely sliced
   onion
1 clove garlic

120 g (4 oz) fat or dripping
salt, pepper
water or stock
30 g (1 oz) flour

Beat the escalopes with a meat hammer. Soften the onion and crushed garlic in the fat, push to one side, add the meat and brown it all over. Stir in salt and pepper and enough stock or water to just cover the meat. Simmer in the covered pan until the meat is tender, adding more liquid if needed. Lift out the meat and keep hot while making the sauce. Sprinkle in the flour and bring to the boil while stirring. Sieve the sauce with its onion and garlic, return it and the escalopes to the pan, and simmer for a few more minutes.

To make BEEF ROLLS prepare the meat as above. Spread each escalope with French mustard. Cover with one or two rashers of fat bacon. Scatter with finely chopped onion and diced pickled cucumber. Roll up like pancakes. Brush with oil, melted fat or dripping. Secure with toothpicks, pack the rolls closely in a casserole and cook in a moderate oven for about 1½ hours until the meat is tender. Baste occasionally adding hot water or stock as needed. Alternatively, the rolls may be cooked in a saucepan with a closely fitting lid. Brown the rolls all over in fat. Add a little water if necessary and cook for about 1 hour.

BEEF ESCALOPE CASSEROLE
GEDÜNSTETE RINDSSCHNITZEL

Prepare the onion and meat as in the recipe for Beef Escalopes (p. 74). Rub the meat with salt and pepper. Grease a casserole and put a layer of onion at the bottom. Cover with a layer of meat and continue thus until both ingredients are used up. Pour in enough milk to cover meat and onions and cook in covered casserole in a moderate oven for about 1½ hours, until the meat is tender. Add a little milk as needed.

BEEF GOULASH   RINDSGULASCH

1 kg (2 lb) stewing beef
240 g (8 oz) finely sliced onion
120 g (4 oz) fat or dripping
1 heaped tablespoon paprika

1 teaspoon sugar
salt, marjoram, caraway seeds
1 dessertspoon vinegar
stock or water

Soften the onion in the fat, push to one side and add the meat, cut into neat pieces as for a stew, with the paprika, salt, sugar, marjoram and caraway seeds. Stir and toss the meat until it is brown all over. Lower the heat a little and continue cooking until the meat 'shrieks'—that is, it makes a hissing noise. Add the vinegar and just enough water to cover the meat. Stew gently in the covered pan until the meat is tender, adding a little more liquid if the meat looks like getting too dry. The gravy should be thick and succulent.

PORK GOULASH   SCHWEINSGULASCH

Use hand of pork. When the meat is tender stir some sour cream into the gravy.

ROAST MINCE LOAF

90 g (3 oz) finely chopped onion
about 30 g (1 oz) finely chopped
parsley
30 g (1 oz) fat or dripping
1¼ kg (3 lb) minced beef or pork

90 g (3 oz) stale white bread,
soaked in water
1 egg
salt, pepper, marjoram
120 g (4 oz) fat

Soften the onion and parsley in the fat and stir together with the meat, the well-squeezed bread, egg, salt, pepper and marjoram. In Vienna the meat loaf is usually made of equal quantities of minced beef and pork. Shape the mixture into a loaf on a floured board, place in a roasting tin, floured side first, pour 120 g (4 oz) hot fat over the meat and roast in a moderately hot oven for about 1 hour, basting several times with the meat juices to which vegetable stock or water can be added after basting. Carefully transfer the meat to a serving dish and keep hot while you make the gravy. Scrape round the bottom of the tin to incorporate all the meat juices, adding a little hot water or stock if needed. Skim off as much fat as possible and serve separately with the meat.

For MEAT RISSOLES (FASCHIERTE LABERLN), make a mixture as above, form into slightly flattened rissoles on a floured board. Fry in fairly hot fat, floured side first, until nicely browned all over. Make gravy as in the recipe for Meat Loaf and serve separately with the hot rissoles. Both Meat Loaf and Rissoles can be eaten cold.

PORK GOULASH WITH SAUERKRAUT

Cook a Pork Goulash (p. 75) until the meat is nearly tender. Stir in sauerkraut—in the proportion of 240 g (8 oz) sauerkraut to 1 kg (2 lb) meat—and very little stock or water, and continue stewing in the covered pan until the meat is tender. Stir sour cream and tomato purée into the gravy.

LAMB GOULASH   SCHÖPSENGULASCH

Use boned shoulder of lamb cut into pieces as for a stew. When the meat is tender stir some tomato purée and sour cream into the gravy.

BEEF AND SAUSAGE STEW   POT-AU-FEU

*480 g (1 lb) shin of beef, cut up
  for a stew*
*240 g (8 oz) Polish boiling ring,
  thickly sliced*
180 g (6 oz) sliced onion
*240 g (8 oz) carrots, thickly
  sliced*

*240 g (8 oz) white cabbage,
  shredded*
480 g (1 lb) potatoes
about 1l (2 pints) water
salt, pepper

Put the meat and vegetables, apart from the potatoes, into the boiling salted water. Cover, and stew until the meat is nearly tender. Add the peeled and quartered potatoes and continue boiling until all ingredients are cooked. Add salt and pepper to taste.

STUFFED PEPPERS   GEFÜLLTE PAPRIKA

*6 large sweet peppers
finely chopped onion
finely chopped parsley
30 g (1 oz) fat
60 g (2 oz) boiled rice*

*240 g ($\frac{1}{2}$ lb) raw minced beef
1 egg
salt
8$\frac{1}{2}$ dl (1$\frac{1}{2}$ pints) tomato sauce*

Cut a slice off the top of each pepper, to serve as a lid. Empty both the peppers and the lids of all pips. Blanch with boiling water, and leave immersed in the water for about 10 minutes. Meanwhile make the stuffing: gently fry a little onion and parsley in the fat, and stir them into the minced beef, together with the lightly beaten egg, salt and rice. Stuff the peppers, put on the lids and secure with wooden toothpicks or with string. Pack tightly in a pan or in a casserole, pour the tomato sauce over and bake in a moderately hot oven for 45 minutes, when the peppers should have changed colour and feel soft when pricked with a fork. If you prefer to do so, the peppers can be cooked on top of the cooker in a heavy pan with a well fitting lid. Boil gently and check occasionally whether more liquid is needed. This dish can be re-heated over steam or in a bain-marie in the oven. Serve with rice.

LAMB RISOTTO   SCHÖPSENPILAW

1 kg (2 lb) boned shoulder of   240 g (8 oz) chopped onion
   lamb   240 g (8 oz) long grain rice
150 g (5 oz) fat rashers of bacon   salt, peppper

Cover the bottom of an ovenproof casserole with rashers of bacon—I use the cheap irregular pieces some grocers sell—and cover the bacon with thick slices of lamb. Sprinkle the meat with salt and pepper and cover with a layer of onion, which in turn is covered with a layer of rice. Continue thus until meat, any remaining bacon, rice and onion are used up. Pour in enough vegetable stock or water to cover the ingredients and cook in the covered casserole until the meat is tender. Add more liquid as needed.

BRAISED SHOULDER OF LAMB WITH
SOUR CREAM SAUCE   GEDÜNSTETE SCHÖPSENSCHULTER

½ shoulder of lamb   salt, pepper
120 g (4 oz) each: 120 g (4 oz) fat or dripping
    carrots   30 g (1 oz) flour
    parsnip   ¼ dl (2 oz) red wine, or wine
    celery   vinegar/water/sugar
    onion   substitute
1 bay leaf   1 dl (4 oz) sour cream
mixed herbs

Melt the fat in the roasting pan in which the meat will be cooked. Add all the chopped or sliced vegetables to the pan and gently fry them in the oven heat. Rub the shoulder of lamb with salt, pepper, bay leaf and chopped fresh or dried herbs. Place the meat on the vegetables and roast in a moderately hot oven until tender. Baste from time to time with the juices in the tin, adding a little vegetable stock or water if needed. Remove the fully cooked meat from the oven and keep hot while you make the sauce. Transfer all the contents of the roasting pan, with a little boiling water added, to a saucepan. Dust with flour and stir and cook for a few moments. Add a little water or stock, bring to the boil while scraping vigorously round the bottom of the pan, and simmer for a few moments. Pass the sauce through a sieve or blend in a liquidizer. Stir in the sour cream and the wine or substitute. Bring back to the boil while stirring, simmer for a few moments and pour the sauce over the meat in the roasting pan. Return to the oven for 5 to 10 minutes.

LAMB AND TOMATO CASSEROLE
GEDÜNSTETES SCHÖPSENFLEISCH MIT PARADEIS

½ boned shoulder of lamb	480 g (1 lb) tomatoes
120 g (4 oz) fat bacon	1 clove of garlic
60 g (2 oz) finely sliced onion	salt, pepper

Put rashers of bacon, or diced bacon, into a casserole and gently fry with the onion in the oven heat. Cut the meat into thick slices, rub with salt, pepper and the crushed garlic and transfer the slices to the casserole, together with halved or thickly sliced tomatoes. Cook in the covered casserole in a moderately hot oven for about 2 hours, adding vegetable stock or water if needed. When the meat is fully cooked keep it hot while you make the sauce. Pass the gravy, with its tomatoes, through a sieve, or put in an electric blender. Season to taste. Thicken the sauce with a little cornflour, bring to the boil, return to the casserole with the meat to heat in the oven for another 5 minutes.

PORK CHOPS WITH MUSHROOMS
SCHWEINSKOTELETTEN MIT SCHWÄMMEN

6 pork chops	150 g (5 oz) sliced mushrooms
60 g (2 oz) fat	salt, pepper

Rub some salt and pepper into the chops, dredge one side with flour and fry them in hot fat, floured side first, until brown all over, lower the heat and continue cooking until the meat is cooked through. Keep the chops hot while the mushrooms are gently fried in the fat. Pile some mushrooms on each chop, pour a few drops of boiling water into the pan, quickly stir around to loosen the meat juices. Pour a little of the gravy over each chop. Serve immediately.

Instead of mushrooms, fry chopped herbs in the fat and pile on top of the chops, making PORK CHOPS WITH HERBS (KRÄUTERKOTEL-LETTEN).

LEG OF PORK WITH MUSTARD SAUCE
SCHWEINSSCHLEGEL MIT SENFSOSS

About 8 servings

1½ kg (3 lb) skinned leg of pork	30 g (1 oz) fat
paprika, salt, caraway seeds	stock or water for basting
90 g (3 oz) fat bacon rashers	2 tablespoons French mustard
90 g (3 oz) finely chopped onion	1 dl (4 oz) sour cream

Rub the skinned leg of pork with the paprika and caraway seeds. Cover with bacon rashers tied on with string. Place in a baking tin on top of the onion which has been softened in the fat. Roast in a moderately hot oven for about 2 hours, until the meat is fully cooked. Baste frequently with its own juice and vegetable stock, or water. When the meat is cooked, keep it hot while quickly making the sauce. Skim off as much fat as possible, scrape round the bottom of the pan to incorporate all meat juices and stir in the mustard and sour cream. Add salt if needed. Bring to the boil and stir and simmer for a few moments. Serve the sauce separately with the meat.

WIENER SCHNITZEL

180 g (6 oz) per person of veal or pork escalopes	about 240 g (8 oz) homemade breadcrumbs
2–4 eggs	salt
flour	

Escalopes should be cut about 5 mm (¼ in) thick and as large as possible from a leg of veal or pork. Make several nicks round the edge of each escalope (and if using pork cut off all fat) and pound with a meat hammer to about half their original thickness. Rub in some salt and dredge all over with flour. Whisk the eggs lightly in a bowl and dip in an escalope held by one corner with a fork. See it is covered with egg all over. Have ready in a large clean bowl, or on a large sheet of paper, a thick layer of breadcrumbs on which you lay the escalope. Toss back and forth until the escalope is breadcrumbed all over. Do not touch by hand or pat down the breadcrumbs. Again holding the escalope with a fork by one corner, place it on a board. Continue flouring, egging and bread-crumbing the remainder of the meat. Heat the fat in a heavy pan and when it is hot lower an escalope into it. Fry golden brown on both sides, lower the heat a little, cover the pan and cook for a few minutes. Lift out with a fork, let the surplus fat drip back and keep the escalope hot while frying the others. As many as will lie flat in the pan without overlapping can be fried at once. They may be kept hot before serving for up to $\frac{1}{2}$ hour. When ready to serve pile the escalopes on a flat serving dish and decorate with sprigs of parsley and slices of lemon. Serve with cucumber salad and potato salad.

PARIS SCHNITZEL   PARISER SCHNITZEL

veal or pork escalopes
flour

eggs
salt, pepper

Follow the preparation of the meat in the recipe for Wiener Schnitzel (p. 80). Dredge all over with flour, then, holding the escalope with a fork by one corner, dip into egg beaten with salt and pepper. Fry the escalopes in hot fat. Serve within 10 minutes.

ESCALOPES NATURE   NATURSCHNITZEL

180 g (6 oz) per person of veal
or pork escalopes

flour
salt, pepper

The escalopes should be cut and prepared as for Wiener Schnitzel

(p. 80). Rub the escalopes with a little salt and pepper, dredge one side with flour and fry in melted fat or butter, floured side first, until they are golden brown all over. Then, only just cover the meat with hot vegetable stock or water, scrape round the bottom of the pan with a fork to incorporate all the meat juices, cover the pan and cook gently for about 5 minutes.

ANCHOVY ESCALOPES SARDELLENSCHNITZEL

Follow the recipes for Escalopes Nature (p. 81) up to the point when the meat has been fried. Only just cover the escalopes with beef bouillon or water, and simmer briefly in a covered pan. Lift out the escalopes and keep hot while you stir sieved or very finely chopped anchovy fillets, or anchovy concentrate, into the stock. Stir vigorously while bringing to the boil, return the meat to the pan. Simmer for a few more moments and serve the escalopes in the sauce.

ESCALOPES AU GRATIN GRATINIERTE SCHNITZEL

about 1 kg (2 lb) of veal or pork, making 10 escalopes
120 g (4 oz) fat
240 g (8 oz) carrots or runner beans
120 g (4 oz) sliced mushrooms
flour

For the sauce:
120 g (4 oz) butter or margarine

60 g (2 oz) flour
1½ dl (5 oz) milk
60 g (2 oz) grated Parmesan or other cheese
1 egg, separated
salt, pepper
30 g (1 oz) homemade breadcrumbs
30 g (1 oz) butter or margarine

Boil the carrots or beans, and dice. Keep their cooking water. Cook the sliced mushrooms in 30 g (1 oz) butter or margarine. Cook the meat as for Escalopes Nature (p. 81), using the vegetable stock. Keep meat and vegetables hot while you make a sauce from the butter, flour, milk, grated cheese, the gravy from the escalopes and seasonings. When the sauce has cooled down a little, stir in an egg yolk. Coat the bottom of an ovenproof dish with a little of the sauce and place a layer of meat on it. Top this with a layer of vegetable coated in sauce. Continue thus until the meat and vegetables have been used up, but keep some of the sauce and fold a stiffly beaten white of egg into it. Spread this over the top, sprinkle with breadcrumbs, dot with flakes of butter and bake in a hot oven for about 15 minutes, until the top has risen and is lightly browned. Serve at once.

ESCALOPES HOLSTEIN

Follow the recipe for Escalopes Nature (p. 81) but pour on only enough boiling water to loosen the meat juices from the bottom of the pan and moisten the escalopes. Keep the meat hot while preparing the garnish. Place a fried egg on top of each escalope. Around the egg arrange rolled-up tinned fillets of anchovy and diced gherkins. Instead of the anchovy, smoked salmon can be used. Serve at once.

PAPRIKA SCHNITZEL

Follow the recipe for Escalopes Nature (p. 81) for preparing and cooking the escalopes. Lift the meat out of the stock, and keep hot while preparing the sauce. Gently fry finely chopped onion in fat, dust with flour and a dessertspoon or more of paprika and cook and stir over a low heat for a few moments. Pour on the stock from the pan in which the meat has been cooked to make a smooth sauce. Stir in some sour cream. Taste, and add salt and paprika if needed. Return the meat to the sauce, and simmer for a few moments before serving.

ESCALOPES IN SOUR CREAM   RAHMSCHNITZEL

Follow the recipe for Escalopes Nature (p. 81). Lift the cooked escalopes out of the pan and keep hot while you stir sour cream into the gravy. Bring to the boil while stirring and pour over the escalopes in the serving dish.

ESCALOPES NATURE WITH VEGETABLE GARNISH

NATURSCHNITZEL MIT GEMÜSEN

veal or *pork escalopes*
salt, pepper, flour

diced carrots, sliced runner beans,
sprigs of cauliflower, peas, all
boiled in slightly salted water
sliced mushrooms cooked in butter

Follow the recipe for Escalopes Nature (p. 81). When the escalopes have been fried, pour over some of the hot stock in which the vegetables have been boiled. Add the vegetables to the meat in the pan, and simmer just long enough to re-heat the vegetables.

VEAL or PORK 'BIRDS'

KALBSVÖGERLN

about 1 kg (2 lb) of veal or *pork*
 leg, cut into escalopes, each
 about 120 g (4 oz)
flour
90 g (3 oz) fat rashers of bacon
60 g (2 oz) finely chopped onion

1 section garlic
180 g (6 oz) raw minced bee,
egg
salt, pepper
120 g (4 oz) fat
1 dl (4 oz) sour cream

If you use pork cut off all the fat round the edges of the meat. Beat the escalopes with a meat hammer to no more than 5 mm ($\frac{1}{4}$ in) thickness. Dip one side into flour. For the filling, gently fry the diced bacon with the onion and the crushed garlic. Stir together with the minced meat and the egg, and season to taste. Spread half the unfloured side of each escalope with this mixture and roll and fold tightly into little parcels. Secure them with string or with toothpicks. The Viennese name for this dish means 'little birdies', and indeed they look like little plucked birds. Pack the 'birds' tightly into an oven dish or a casserole, in which the fat has been melted, and roast in a moderately hot oven for about 1 hour. Baste frequently with their own juices to which vegetable stock or water can be added. When the meat is fully cooked, stir sour cream into the gravy, baste the little birds again, and return to the oven for another 5 minutes.

For BEEF 'BIRDS' (RINDSVÖGERLN) use blade of beef cut into escalopes, instead of pork or veal, but the cooking time will be about ½ hour longer.

MEAT AND VEGETABLE PUDDING
FLEISCH–UND GEMÜSEDUNSTKOCH

240 g (8 oz) stewing veal or
  hand of pork
120 g (4 oz) each:
    turnip
    carrots
    runner beans
    small brussels sprouts

120 g (4 oz) peas
150 g (5 oz) butter or margarine
3 eggs, separated
salt, pepper
150 g (5 oz) homemade
  breadcrumbs

Stew the diced meat with the diced turnip and carrot in slightly salted water until about half-cooked. Add the sliced and chopped runner beans and the tiny sprouts, and continue cooking until the meat is tender. Add the peas and cook for another couple of minutes. Strain—keep the stock to use another time. Cream the butter with the egg yolks, stir in the meat and vegetables and season to taste. Fold in the stiffly beaten whites of egg together with the breadcrumbs. Transfer the mixture to a large, greased and floured pudding basin, secure the top and steam for 40 minutes. As soon as possible, turn out and serve with a mushroom or cheese sauce.

VEAL or PORK RISOTTO
REISFLEISCH

720 g (1¼ lb) stewing veal or
  hand of pork
60 g (2 oz) fat bacon rashers
120 g (4 oz) finely chopped onion
salt, paprika

240 g (8 oz) long grain rice
90 g (3 oz) fat
60 g (2 oz) grated Parmesan or
  Cheddar cheese

Gently fry the onion and diced bacon, push to one side and melt the fat. Add the meat cut into neat pieces, as for a stew, and continue cooking over a low heat until the meat is browned all over and half-cooked—20–30 minutes. Add the rice and seasonings. Fry, stirring and tossing until the rice is beginning to be transparent. Pour in cold vegetable stock or water to about 5 cm (2 in) above the level of the food. Bring to the boil and cook gently in the covered pan until the meat is tender and the rice has absorbed most of the liquid—20–30 minutes. With a fork stir in lightly about two-thirds of the grated cheese; sprinkle the remaining cheese over the risotto in the serving dish.

Instead of cooking the risotto in a saucepan on top of the cooker, once the stock is in, it can be cooked in a casserole in the oven.

VEAL or PORK STEW IN WHITE SAUCE
EINGEMACHTES KALBFLEISCH

About 8 servings

1 kg (2 lb) stewing veal or hand
of pork
120 g (4 oz) fat
240 g (8 oz) each:
   cooked sprigs of
      cauliflower
   cooked, diced carrots
   cooked peas

120 g (4 oz) sliced mushrooms,
   cooked in butter or margarine
salt, pepper
vegetable stock or water

For the white sauce:
120 g (4 oz) butter or margarine
60 g (2 oz) flour
about 2½ dl (½ pint) of milk

Cut the meat into neat pieces and brown all over in the fat. Add salt and pepper, just cover the meat with vegetable stock or water and boil gently in a covered pan until tender, adding more water if necessary. Keep the meat hot while you make a smooth sauce from the butter or margarine, flour, milk, meat juices and stock in the pan, with seasoning to taste. Bring to the boil and add the meat and all the vegetables to the sauce. Simmer for a few minutes. Little Breadcrumb Dumplings (p. 62) are often added to the sauce.

SCRAMBLED BRAINS
GERÖSTETES HIRN

2 sets of ox brains
finely chopped onion
finely chopped parsley

120 g (4 oz) butter or margarine
salt, pepper

Brains in this country are comparatively cheap—in Vienna they are as expensive as liver and kidneys. So make the most of the variety of ways they can be served!

Soak the brains for at least 10 minutes in cold water. Drain. Discard the skins, clots of blood and any bone splinters. Immerse the brains in boiling water to which a little vinegar has been added and boil for 2 minutes. Drain. Soften some onion and parsley in the fat, push to one side and add the brains, cut up very small. Add salt and pepper and scramble with a fork until the brains are thoroughly cooked—about 10 minutes. Serve as soon as possible. Before serving, 120 g (4 oz) of browned butter can be poured over the brains. If you wish, add 2–4 lightly beaten eggs while scrambling.

BRAINS FRIED IN BREADCRUMBS

GEBACKENES HIRN

2 sets of brains
2 or 3 eggs
salt, pepper

flour
homemade breadcrumbs

Prepare and boil the brains following the method for Scrambled Brains (p. 86). Cut the brains into 1 cm (½ in) slices. Dredge with flour, dip into egg lightly beaten with salt and pepper, and coat with breadcrumbs. Fry in hot fat until golden brown. Serve as soon as possible with a green salad.

BRAINS AU GRATIN

GRATINIERTES HIRN

1 set of brains
60 g (2 oz) butter
finely chopped parsley
30 g (1 oz) margarine
anchovy concentrate

30 g (1 oz) homemade
breadcrumbs
30 g (1 oz) grated Parmesan or
Cheddar cheese

Follow the method for Scrambled Brains (p. 86) in preparing and boiling the brains. Grease 10 scallop shells with the margarine creamed with enough anchovy concentrate to give a strong flavour. If shells are not available use small ovenproof dishes such as ramekins. Gently fry parsley in the butter, add the cooked brains, cut up very small, and fry for a few minutes, with added salt and pepper. Transfer to the shells, sprinkle with breadcrumbs and Parmesan, dot with flakes of butter, and put for a few minutes in a hot oven.

FRIED KIDNEYS AND BRAINS   NIERNDLN UND HIRN

480 g (1 lb) pig's kidneys   *120 g (4 oz) fat*
240 g (8 oz) brains   *salt, pepper, marjoram*
120 g (4 oz) finely chopped onion

Prepare the kidneys and slice. Prepare and boil the brains following the method for Scrambled Brains (p. 86). Soften the onion in the fat, push to one side and quickly brown the kidneys all over. Add the brains, chopped very small, and scramble until they are thoroughly cooked. Lastly, stir in the seasonings. Serve as soon as possible.

BRAISED HEART   GEDÜNSTETES HERZ

720 g (1½ lb) of hearts—ox   *about 2½ dl (½ pint) white wine,*
  heart, or 3 lamb's, or calf's or   *or wine vinegar/sugar/water*
  pig's hearts   *substitute*
60 g (2 oz) fat bacon rashers   *2 tablespoons tomato purée*
120 g (4 oz) fat or dripping   *90 g (3 oz) sliced mushrooms*
120 g (4 oz) finely sliced onion   *30 g (1 oz) flour*
                                      salt, pepper

Cut the heart or hearts in half, wash out all congealed blood and cut out the ligaments and cartilage. Cut the meat into 1 cm (½ in) slices. Gently fry the onion with the diced bacon in the fat. Push to one side, add the meat and brown it all over. Sprinkle in the flour, and stir and cook for a few moments. Add salt and pepper while stirring. Pour in the wine or vinegar substitute, the mushrooms and tomato purée. Bring to the boil while stirring, and simmer in the covered pan until tender, about 1½ hours. Add more liquid and salt and pepper as needed.

SWEET AND SOUR LIGHTS WITH DUMPLINGS
BEUSCHEL UND KNÖDEL

This is a Viennese speciality, a rather coarse dish, though quite acceptable at long intervals. My husband enjoys it, but it's not a dish I would choose to serve at a dinner party!

300 g (10 oz) lights	*1 dessertspoon pickling spice*
300 g (10 oz) heart	*1 tablespoon vinegar*
90 g (3 oz) each:	*salt and pepper*
parsnip	*lemon juice*
carrots	*120 g (4 oz) fat*
celery	*120 g (4 oz) finely sliced onion*
6 peppercorns	*120 g (4 oz) flour*
1 bayleaf	*2 sugar lumps*

Boil the lights and heart, with the roughly cut up carrot, celery and parsnip, in salted water, to which peppercorns, pickling spice, bay leaf and vinegar have been added, until the meat is tender. Strain and keep the stock. Allow the meat to get cold then cut into thin strips about 2½ cm (1 in) long. Make a roux from the fat, in which the sugar has been lightly browned with the onion, and the flour. Pour on the meat and vegetable stock and bring to the boil while stirring. Add the meat, lemon juice, salt and pepper to taste and simmer in a covered pan for about 15 minutes. Serve with Bread Dumplings (p. 61).

LIVER FRIED IN BREADCRUMBS
GEBACKENE LEBER

720 (1½ lb) pig's or calf's liver	*homemade breadcrumbs*
flour	*salt*
eggs	

Cut the liver into 1 cm (½ in) thick slices, dredge all over with flour, dip into egg lightly beaten with salt, and coat with breadcrumbs. Fry in hot fat or oil until golden brown. Serve as soon as possible, piled on a dish and decorated with slices of lemon.

TYROLEAN LIVER

720 g (1½ lb) liver
30 g (1 oz) flour
120 g (4 oz) fat
120 g (4 oz) finely chopped onion
2½ dl (½ pint) stock or water

1 dl (4 oz) sour cream
15 g (½ oz) capers
1 teaspoon vinegar
salt, pepper

Gently fry the onion in the fat. Cut the liver into slices about 5 mm (¼ in) thick. Dredge one side with flour and fry, floured side first, until browned both sides. Pour on the water or vegetable stock and bring to the boil, stirring vigorously to incorporate all the meat juices from the bottom of the pan. Stir in the sour cream, capers, vinegar, and salt and pepper to taste. Stir and simmer for a few moments before serving at once.

SWEETBREADS IN SOUR CREAM

1 kg (2 lb) sweetbreads
60 g (2 oz) fat bacon rashers
salt, pepper
60 g (2 oz) each:
   carrots
   parsnip

60 g (2 oz) celery
60 g (2 oz) fat
vegetable stock or water
½ dl (2 oz) white wine or
   vinegar/sugar/water substitute
1 dl (4 oz) sour cream

Blanch the sweetbreads and leave them in the water for a few minutes. Drain. Plunge into cold water and drain again. Slice them and cut out edges of skin and mottlings of blood. Gently fry the roughly chopped vegetables and the diced bacon in the fat, push to one side and add the sweetbreads. Continue frying and stirring until they are lightly browned all over. Add salt and pepper, the wine or its substitute and enough vegetable stock or water to cover the meat. Cook gently in a covered pan on top of the cooker, or in a casserole in a moderately hot oven for about 15 minutes, until the sweetbreads are tender. Keep the meat hot while you put the gravy and vegetables through a sieve or blend in a liquidizer. Stir the sour cream into the sauce, adjust the seasoning, and add the meat to the sauce. Stir and simmer for a few more moments.

TONGUE WITH SWEETBREAD SAUCE

ZUNGENRAGOUT

About 8–10 servings

1 fresh ox tongue	*120 g (4 oz) butter or margarine*
120 g (4 oz) chopped celery	*45 g (1½ oz) flour*
120 g (4 oz) finely chopped onion	*salt, pepper*
240 g (8 oz) sweetbreads	*chopped parsley*
120 g (4 oz) sliced mushrooms	

Boil the tongue with the onion and celery in unsalted water—this could take anywhere between 3–6 hours. When the tongue is fully cooked the little bones at the throat end pull out easily. Peel the tongue and keep it hot in its stock. Boil the sweetbreads for 10 minutes in slightly salted water. Drain. Cut off and discard as much of the thick skins as possible. Slice the sweetbreads and gently fry with the mushrooms in the butter. Add salt and pepper and dust with flour. Stir and cook for a few moments. Pour on about 2½ dl (½ pint) of the tongue stock, and simmer, stirring, for a few minutes. Adjust seasoning. If you wish, stir some sour cream into the sauce. Arrange thick slices of tongue in a serving dish and pour the sweetbread sauce over. Sprinkle with chopped parsley.

CHICKEN FRIED IN BREADCRUMBS

BACKHENDL

This is a Viennese speciality, and rightly very popular. There are some restaurants, mainly around Vienna, who call themselves *Backhendl Stationen* where these little fried chickens are the only meat dish on the menu. Choose small spring chickens, which used to be available only for a short season, from April until the autumn, but which now, thanks to the deep-freezer, can be had all the year round—though I still prefer the fresh ones. They should not weigh more than about 480 g (1 lb) each.

3 small chickens, jointed	*homemade breadcrumbs*
salt	*eggs*
flour	*fat or oil for frying*

Rub everything, including livers, hearts and gizzards, with salt.

Dredge with flour, dip in egg and coat with breadcrumbs. Do not touch the pieces by hand when coating them with the crumbs, and do not pat down. Heat the fat in a strong pan to deep-frying temperature. Carefully immerse as many pieces of chicken as will lie flat without overlapping. Fry golden brown all over (roughly 3 minutes), lower the heat a little, cover the pan and allow to cook a little longer to make sure the meat is cooked through (roughly 5 minutes). Prick with a fork to test that they are fully cooked. Lift out by one corner with a fork and let surplus fat drip back. Keep hot while frying the remaining pieces. The chicken are best eaten at once but they can be kept hot, covered with foil, in a slow oven or in the hot cupboard of the cooker for up to 20 minutes. Serve piled on a dish decorated with sprigs of parsley which can also be fried crisp in the hot fat, and with slices of lemon. Serve with a green salad or a cucumber salad and a potato salad.

PAPRIKA CHICKEN   PAPRIKA HENDL

1 jointed chicken, about 1½ kg (3 lb)	*1 heaped tablespoon paprika*
	30 g (1 oz) flour
90 g (3 oz) fat bacon	*1 dl (4 oz) sour cream*
120 g (4 oz) finely chopped onion	*salt*

Gently fry the diced bacon over a low heat with the onion. Push to one side and fry the chicken pieces until they have changed colour. Add the paprika and some salt, and toss and fry a little longer. Add enough vegetable stock or water to cover the meat and simmer steadily in a covered pan until the chicken is tender. Lift out the chicken and keep hot while you make the sauce: sprinkle the flour into the stock while stirring vigorously to loosen all the meat juices from the bottom of the pan. Stir and boil to dissolve all lumps of flour. Stir in the sour cream, taste and adjust seasoning. Return the chicken pieces to the sauce and simmer and stir for a few minutes. Serve with Flour or Egg Dumplings (p. 63) or Rice (p. 70).

CHICKEN RISOTTO   HÜHNERREIS

1 jointed chicken	*120 g (4 oz) chicken giblets*

120 g (4 oz) chicken livers	*2 cups long grain rice*
120 g (4 oz) mushrooms	*salt, pepper*
60 g (2 oz) butter	*60 g (2 oz) grated Parmesan or*
120 g (4 oz) fat	*Cheddar cheese*
120 g (4 oz) onion	

Simmer the chicken and giblets in 1 l (2 pints) slightly salted water until tender. Strain into a bowl. Keep the chicken hot. Soften the finely sliced onion in the fat, push to one side and add the rice. Fry gently and toss until the rice is beginning to be transparent. Add salt and pepper and 4 cups of the strained chicken stock. Bring to the boil and boil gently in the covered pan until all the liquid has been absorbed by the rice, when it will be cooked. Keep hot over steam. Fry the sliced mushrooms and liver in the butter and mix them lightly into the rice. Use a fork for mixing and take care not to crush the grains of rice. Mix in the grated Parmesan. Slice the chicken hearts and gizzards, take the meat off the bone and cut into neat pieces and mix them all lightly into the rice. If the risotto is at all dry, add a little chicken stock.

Substitute boiled diced ham for HAM RISOTTO (SCHINKENREIS).

Substitute sliced chicken livers cooked in butter for CHICKEN LIVER RISOTTO (HÜHNERLEBERREIS).

Prawn, crayfish and mussels, coated with white sauce are used for SEAFOOD RISOTTO. The Viennese version of this last dish would be made with river crayfish (KREBSEN RISOTTO).

CHICKEN IN SOUR CREAM HUHN IN RAHMSOSS

Soften sliced onion in margarine, push to one side and add chicken joints and chopped gizzard and heart. Fry over a low heat until lightly browned. Season, sprinkle with flour and cook and stir for a few moments. Add enough stock or water to cover the meat and cook in the covered pan until the meat is tender. Stir sour cream into the sauce.

CHICKEN IN WHITE SAUCE   EINMACHHUHN

*1 jointed chicken, about 1½ kg
(3 lb), with giblets
60 g (2 oz) each:*
    *parsnip
    celery
    carrots
    onion
120 g (4 oz) margarine or dripping*

*salt, pepper
120 g (4 oz) small sprigs of
    cooked cauliflower*

For the white sauce:
*90 g (3 oz) butter or margarine
45 g (1½ oz) flour
120 g (4 oz) mushrooms*

Gently fry the sliced onion and the other roughly chopped vegetables in 120 g (4 oz) fat. Push to one side and add the chicken joints and the chopped heart and gizzard with salt and pepper. Gently brown the meat all over. Cover with vegetable stock or water and simmer in the covered pan until tender. Strain into a bowl and discard the vegetables. Keep the chicken hot while you make the sauce: cook the sliced mushrooms and chicken liver in the butter, dust with flour, and cook over a low heat for a few moments. Pour on the chicken stock and bring to the boil while stirring smooth. Season to taste. Add the chicken joints and the cauliflower. Simmer for a few minutes before serving. Small Breadcrumb Dumplings (p. 62) may be added to the sauce.

GOOSE, or CHICKEN or HAM WITH BARLEY
RITSCHERT

This is a Viennese Jewish dish, which should really be made with legs of goose. Goose, however, seems very hard to get in this country and I have successfully varied the dish with the ingredients given below.

*240 g (8 oz) goose or duck or
    chicken or ham
150 (5 oz) haricot beans
150 g (5 oz) pearl barley
120 g (4 oz) finely chopped onion
finely chopped parsley*

*90 g (3 oz) fat or dripping
45 g (1½ oz) flour
bean stock
salt, pepper*

Soak the beans overnight. Boil the beans with the barley until tender. (This takes at least 1 hour.) Drain. Roast or stew the meat, take it off the bone and dice. Soften the onion and parsley in the fat, stir in the flour, salt and pepper and continue cooking over a low heat for a few moments. Pour on sufficient bean-stock to make a thick sauce, stir and smooth. Transfer the meat, beans, barley and sauce to a covered casserole and cook in a moderate oven for about 40 minutes. The consistency should be moist. Add more liquid if needed but avoid it being runny. *Ritschert* is actually improved by being re-heated, and for that reason I always cook it the previous day.

GOOSE LIVER
GANSLEBER

This is a true delicacy. Put it with its fat around it in a small oven-proof dish in a moderately hot oven until all the fat is liquid and the liver is cooked. Let it get cold. Spread the fat on slices of toast or fresh brown bread, put slices of liver on top and sprinkle with salt. Formerly, when geese were forcibly fed until their livers became diseased, these goose livers were very big. Now that this cruel treatment has been banned in most countries the livers are quite small, but are still worth baking separately from the goose itself.

ROAST HARE WITH SOUR CREAM SAUCE
HASENBRATEN MIT RAHMSOSS

1 hare, unjointed but with head and tail removed
150 g (5 oz) rashers of fat bacon
fat or dripping
60 g (2 oz) each:
    carrots
    parsnip
    celery
    onion
stock

30 g (1 oz) flour
salt, pepper, mixed herbs, 1 bayleaf
1 dessertspoon redcurrant or cranberry jelly
1 dl (4 oz) red wine or wine vinegar/sugar/water/substitute
1 dl 4 (oz) sour cream
dash of lemon juice

Gently fry all the chopped vegetables in melted fat in the roasting pan in which the hare will be cooked. Wrap the hare in rashers of bacon, secure with string and place on top of the vegetables. Add a little stock or water and roast in a moderately hot oven for about 1 hour, basting frequently. Keep the hare hot while you make the sauce. Pour on a very little boiling water and scrape vigorously round the pan to incorporate all the meat juices. Dust with flour and bring to the boil while stirring. Put the sauce through a sieve or in an electric blender. Return to the pan, stir in salt and all the spices and herbs, add the red wine or substitute, lemon juice and sour cream. Bring to the boil while stirring, simmer for about 5 minutes. Remove the bacon from the hare, place it whole or jointed in a deep serving dish and either pour the sauce over or serve separately. The bacon can be arranged round the hare.

RABBIT may be cooked the same way. The meat may also be jointed, or even removed from the bone after it is cooked and then returned to the sauce, to be simmered for a few more minutes.

PHEASANT CASSEROLE   FASAN GEDÜNSTET

1 pheasant	*60 g (2 oz) celery*
60 g (2 oz) bacon rashers	*1 onion*
salt	*fat*
60 g (2 oz) each:	*5½ dl (1 pint) stock*
parsnip	*45 g (1½ oz) flour*
carrots	*1 dl(4 oz) sour cream*

Melt some fat in the casserole or roasting tin in which the pheasant will be cooked, chop all the vegetables and soften them in the fat. Rub the pheasant all over with salt. Cover the breast and legs with rashers of bacon—secure them with string or with wooden tooth-picks. Place the bird on top of the vegetables. Add about ½ l (1 pint) of clear beef or vegetable stock and cook in the covered baking tin or casserole in a moderately hot oven for about 1 hour. Baste once or twice with the juices in the casserole (a little more liquid can be added after basting). When the bird is tender keep it hot while making the sauce. Sprinkle the flour into the gravy, bring to the boil while stirring and cook for a few moments. Add a little boiling water and boil and stir to incorporate all meat juices in the pan. Pass the sauce through a sieve or put in an electric blender. Bring it to the boil again, stir in the sour cream and simmer for a few moments. Taste, and add a little salt if needed. Pour the sauce over the carved pheasant in the serving dish and return to the oven for a few more minutes.

PARTRIDGE and PIGEON may be cooked the same way, though for a shorter time, of course.

VENISON CASSEROLE   GEDÜNSTETES WILD

1 kg (2 lb) venison, cut up for a stew	salt, pepper, mixed herbs, bayleaf, grated nutmeg
90 g (3 oz) each:	stock
parsnip	30 g (1 oz) flour
carrots	2 tablespoons red wine or wine
celery	vinegar/sugar/water substitute
onion	1 dl (4 oz) sour cream
fat or dripping	dash of lemon juice

Gently fry all the chopped vegetables in the fat. Push to one side and fry the meat pieces until they are browned all over. Stir in salt, pepper, herbs and nutmeg. Add enough vegetable stock or water to cover the meat and cook in a casserole in the oven, or in a covered pan on top of the cooker until the meat is tender. (Add more liquid if needed, so it is not allowed to dry out.) Keep the meat hot while you make the sauce. If there is still a lot of liquid in the pan reduce the quantity by boiling rapidly—you should be aiming to finish the dish with a thick rich sauce. Sprinkle in the flour, bring to the boil while stirring. Pass the gravy together with the vegetables through a sieve or put in an electric blender. Stir in the wine or substitute, the sour cream and lemon juice. Return the meat to the sauce, adjust the taste and simmer in the covered pan for about 5 minutes.

ROAST VENISON   GEBRATENER REHRÜCKEN ODER SCHLEGEL

About 8 servings

> 2 kg (4 lb) venison, leg or
>   saddle or shoulder
> 120 g (4 oz) rashers of fat bacon
> fat or dripping
> 90 g (3 oz) each:
>   parsnip
>   carrots
>   celery
>   onion

> 2½ dl (½ pint) stock
> 30 g (1 oz) flour
> salt, pepper, grated nutmeg,
>   mixed herbs, 1 bayleaf
> 1 dl (4 oz) red wine or wine
>   vinegar/sugar/water substitute
> 1 dl (4 oz) sour cream
> 60 g (2 oz) redcurrant or
>   cranberry jelly

Melt the fat and gently fry all the chopped vegetables. Wrap the venison in rashers of bacon and secure with string. Place it on top of the vegetables, add about 3 dl (½ pint) of beef or vegetable stock and roast in a moderately hot oven, basting frequently. When the meat is very nearly tender—probably about 2 hours—remove it from the pan and keep hot while you make the sauce. Skim off as much fat as possible, pour on a little boiling water and vigorously scrape round the pan to incorporate all meat juices. Dust with the flour, bring to the boil while stirring, add the wine or substitute, salt, herbs, spices and redcurrant jelly. Pass through a sieve or an electric blender together with the vegetables, stir in the sour cream and bring the sauce to the boil again while stirring. Simmer for a few moments. Return the meat to the oven pan, remove the bacon, pour the sauce over the meat and return to the oven for about 10 minutes, or until the meat is tender.

Savoury Sauces

I am including here, for handy reference, recipes for those sauces I have mentioned elsewhere in the book in serving suggestions. I would not claim that they are all specifically Viennese.

MAYONNAISE

1 egg yolk	*pepper*
about 1½ dl (4–6 oz) vegetable	*1 dessertspoon vinegar*
oil	*French mustard*
salt	*Worcester sauce*

When making mayonnaise it is essential to have all ingredients at room temperature. Perfectionists use olive oil, but it is really too expensive today if you eat a lot of salads. Put the yolk in a basin and beat it lightly with a little salt and pepper. Stir in an eggspoonful of French mustard. Holding the oil bottle poised over the basin add the oil drop by drop. The next drop must only be added when the previous one has been absorbed by the yolk. Use a wooden or a silver spoon for stirring. Or use an electric mixer at slowest speed. Once the mayonnaise begins to thicken rapidly the oil can be added more quickly, but you must not stop stirring. Once all the oil has been absorbed stir in the vinegar and a drop of Worcester sauce. Taste, and add salt and pepper as needed. If the mayonnaise curdles put it in a clean bowl (so as not to contaminate the new mixture) and stir in 1–2 tablespoons hot vinegar very slowly. This first-aid method usually works. Mayonnaise not used immediately should be kept in a screwtop jar in the refrigerator; it should be taken out about 1 hour before it is needed and stirred.

MAYONNAISE WITH PEPPERS   PAPRIKA MAYONNAISE

Stir into mayonnaise a green pepper, emptied of all pips and cut into fine short strips.

TARTARE SAUCE   TARTARENSOSS

Into mayonnaise stir: 1 gherkin, 1 fillet of anchovy, 10 g ($\frac{1}{4}$ oz) capers, a little onion and a sprig of parsley, all chopped very small. Serve with fish or mushrooms fried in breadcrumbs, or with fried or grilled steak, or with any cold meat or fish.

GREEN MAYONNAISE   GRÜNE MAYONNAISE

Stir some sour cream, chopped gherkins and a little concentrated spinach purée into mayonnaise, just enough to give it a greenish colouring.

RED MAYONNAISE   ROTE MAYONNAISE

Stir in enough concentrated tomato purée to give a pink colouring to the mayonnaise.

VIENNESE ANCHOVY SAUCE   WIENER SARDELLENSOSS

30 g (1 oz) margarine
finely chopped onion
finely chopped parsley
30 g (1 oz) flour
2 or 3 anchovy fillets, chopped
  finely or liquidized

dash of lemon juice
about 2$\frac{1}{2}$ dl ($\frac{1}{2}$ pint) beef bouillon
  or water and bouillon cubes
salt

Soften the onion and parsley in the margarine, dust with the flour and stir for a few moments. Add the liquid and the anchovy fillets, and bring to the boil while stirring. Add a little lemon juice and salt to taste. Stir. Simmer in the covered pan for about 5 minutes. Serve hot with steamed fish, with boiled chicken or beef, and with roast or braised veal, pork or beef.

Savoury Sauces

CAPER SAUCE

finely chopped onion
finely chopped parsley
30 g (1 oz) fat or margarine
15 g ($\frac{1}{2}$ oz) flour

about 2$\frac{1}{2}$ dl ($\frac{1}{2}$ pint) beef bouillon
    or water
60 g (2 oz) chopped capers
salt, pepper

Soften the onion and parsley in the fat, add the flour and cook for a few moments. Pour on the liquid while stirring and cook and stir for a minute. Add the capers, salt and pepper to taste and simmer in the covered pan for 5 minutes. Serve hot with boiled meat and steamed fish.

CHEESE SAUCE

KÄSESOSS

2 eggs
1 tablespoon cornflour
2$\frac{1}{2}$ dl ($\frac{1}{2}$ pint) milk

150 g (5 oz) grated Parmesan or
    Emmental or Gruyère or
    Cheddar cheese
salt, pepper, grated nutmeg

Beat the eggs lightly with the cornflour and some of the milk. Stir until smooth. Stir in the remainder of the milk, the cheese and seasonings. Beat over steam until thick. Serve hot with pasta and steamed savoury puddings.

CHIVES SAUCE I

SCHNITTLAUCHSOSS I

about 2$\frac{1}{2}$ dl ($\frac{1}{2}$ pint) homemade
    mayonnaise
2 hard-boiled egg yolks

30 g (1 oz) stale white bread,
    soaked in vinegar and water
1 heaped tablespoon chopped
    chives

Squeeze out the soaked bread. Pass it through a sieve (or in an electric blender) with the egg yolks. Fold into the mayonnaise together with the chives. Serve with hot or cold boiled beef and with hot or cold steamed fish.

CHIVES SAUCE II

about ½ dl (2 oz) cooled beef
bouillon
2 hard-boiled egg yolks
1 eggspoon cornflour
lemon juice to taste

about ½ dl (2 oz) oil
1 heaped tablespoon chopped
chives
salt, pepper, vinegar

Over heat, beat the sieved egg yolks, cornflour and lemon juice into the bouillon until it thickens. Remove from the heat and stir in the oil drop by drop. Do not add the next drop until the previous one has been stirred in and absorbed. Stir in salt, pepper and vinegar to taste, and finally fold in the chives. Serve cold in the same way as Chives Sauce I (p. 101).

CRANBERRY SAUCE

If you are lucky enough to be able to get fresh cranberries, simmer the berries with the minimum of water and a little sugar, until soft. If fresh cranberries are not available use tinned or frozen berries. Serve cold with game.

CUCUMBER SAUCE

240 g (8 oz) cucumber (ridge
cucumber can be used)
finely chopped onion
finely chopped parsley
60 g (2 oz) butter or margarine

45 g (1½ oz) flour
about 2½ dl (½ pint) beef bouillon
salt, pepper
1 dl (4 oz) sour cream
chopped dill, optional

Cut the peeled cucumber into thin slices, sprinkle with salt and leave for about ½ hour. Soften the onion and parsley in the butter, dust with the flour and cook for a few moments. Add the bouillon and bring to the boil while stirring to dissolve all lumps. Rinse the cucumber under the cold tap and stir into the sauce. Add the sour cream, chopped dill if you wish, and season. Simmer the sauce for a minute. Serve hot with boiled or roast meat.

CUMBERLAND SAUCE

2 tablespoons redcurrant jelly
2 tablespoons redcurrant jam
2 tablespoons apricot jam
juice of 1 lemon
juice of 1 orange

½ teaspoon mustard powder
grated skin of ½ orange
1 dl (4 oz) cheap red wine
salt, pepper

Mix all ingredients. If the apricot jam contains whole fruit pass it through a sieve first. Serve with game.

DILL SAUCE   DILLENSOSS

Fresh dill is not easy to buy in this country. I grow it in the garden, where once sown it spreads like a weed.

60 g (2 oz) butter or margarine
finely chopped onion
1 heaped tablespoonful finely
  chopped parsley
1 heaped tablespoonful finely
  chopped dill

30 g (1 oz) flour
about 2½ dl (½ pint) beef bouillon
salt, vinegar
½ dl (2 oz) sour cream

Soften the onion and parsley in the butter, stir in the flour and cook a little longer while stirring. Add the bouillon and the dill. Bring to the boil, and continue stirring until smooth. Stir in the sour cream, and season to taste. Bring back to the boil and simmer for a moment. Serve hot, with boiled meats and steamed fish.

GARLIC SAUCE   KNOBLAUCHSOSS

3–5 sections garlic, depending on
  size
60 g (2 oz) margarine

60 g (2 oz) flour
about 2½ dl (½ pint) beef bouillon
salt

Crush the garlic with salt. Let it froth in the melted margarine, add the flour, and stir for a few moments. Pour on the beef bouillon, and bring to the boil while stirring. Simmer in the covered pan for 5–10 minutes. Serve hot with roast or boiled lamb or mutton.

Savoury Sauces

MIXED HERBS SAUCE
KRÄUTERSOSS

1 tablespoon each onion, dill,
chives, parsley, marjoram, all
finely chopped
60 g (2 oz) butter or margarine
30 g (1 oz) flour

1 dessertspoon vinegar
salt, pepper
about 2½ dl (½ pint) beef
bouillon or water

Soften the onion and parsley in the butter, add the flour and cook for a few moments. Add the liquid and the other herbs, with salt, pepper and vinegar to taste. Bring to the boil while stirring and simmer for a few minutes. You can substitute any other herbs for those I have suggested. Serve hot with boiled or roast meat or with steamed fish.

HORSERADISH AND APPLE SAUCE
APFELKREN

240 (8 oz) cooking apples
30 g (1 oz) fresh, grated
horseradish

1 tablespoon vinegar
dash of lemon
45 g (1½ oz) sugar

Fresh horseradish is not always easy to get in this country, but I have made the sauce successfully from dried horseradish. Peel and core the apples and boil in very little water to which a dash of lemon juice is added. Pass the apples through a sieve and mix the grated horseradish into the purée. Add vinegar and sugar. Serve the cold sauce with hot boiled beef, gammon or sausages.

MUSHROOM SAUCE
SCHWAMMERLSOSS

120 g (4 oz) mushrooms, sliced
finely chopped onion
finely chopped parsley
60 g (2 oz) butter or margarine
30 g (1 oz) flour

about 2½ dl (½ pint) beef bouillon
or water
½ dl (2 oz) sour cream
salt, pepper
dash of lemon juice

Soften the onion and parsley in the butter over a low heat, add the mushrooms and cook. Dust with the flour and cook for a few moments gently until tender. Add enough liquid to make a thick sauce and cook and stir for a few moments. Add the sour cream and seasonings to taste. Simmer the sauce for a few minutes. Serve hot, with pasta and steamed fish and savoury puddings.

ONION SAUCE ZWIEBELSOSS

120 g (4 oz) fat or margarine   *about 2½ dl (½ pint) beef bouillon*
30 g (1 oz) sugar   *or vegetable stock*
120 g (4 oz) finely sliced onion   *vinegar*
60 g (2 oz) flour   *salt, pepper*

Gently brown the sugar in the fat, add the onion and continue cooking over a low heat until slightly browned. Dust with the flour and stir and cook a little longer. Pour on the stock, and stir while bringing to the boil. Cook in the covered pan for about 10 minutes until the onion is very soft. Pass through a sieve or put in an electric blender. Return to the pan, add salt, pepper and vinegar to taste. Bring to the boil while stirring. Simmer for a moment. Serve hot with boiled meat.

TOMATO SAUCE PARADEISSOSS

480 g (1 lb) tomatoes   *60 g (2 oz) flour*
120 g (4 oz) fat or margarine   *about 2½ dl (½ pint) water*
finely chopped onion   *1 dessertspoon vinegar*
finely chopped parsley   *1 dessertspoon lemon juice*
2 dessertspoons sugar   *salt, pepper*

Although I often use tomato concentrate instead of fresh tomatoes, when tomatoes are reasonably cheap and there is time available I do recommend using fresh ones. A small tin or tube of concentrate equals about 480 g (1 lb) tomatoes, but you must add a little extra water. Soften the onion and parsley in the fat, over a low heat. Add the sugar and let it brown slightly. Add the roughly chopped tomatoes and cook for a few minutes. Stir in flour and cook a little longer. Pour on the water and cook gently in the covered pan for about 5 minutes until the tomatoes are very soft. Pass through a sieve or put in an electric blender. Return to the pan, and add all the seasonings to taste. Stir while bringing to the boil, and simmer for a minute. Serve hot with pasta.

SAUCE VINAIGRETTE   SAURE SOSS

45 g (1½ oz) onion, finely
   chopped
3 gherkins, chopped
30 g (1 oz) capers, chopped
parsley, finely chopped

2 hard-boiled eggs, chopped
½ dl (2 oz) vinegar
1 dl (4 oz) oil
salt, pepper, French mustard,
   dash of Worcester sauce

Make a dressing from the vinegar, salt, mustard, pepper, Worcester sauce and oil, and stir in lightly all the chopped ingredients. Serve with such dishes as cold asparagus, cold roast meat, avocado pears, mussels and cold fish.

Desserts

Desserts are important in Viennese cookery, and meals are usually rounded off with a sweet dish. The distinction between desserts served at main meals and cakes and biscuits served with tea or coffee, at mid-morning or in the afternoon, has become blurred. Obviously, hot sweets which should be served very soon after being cooked or baked are meant to accompany a main meal, as are others which must be eaten with a spoon and fork. On the other hand, most cakes and some biscuits can be served at any time. I would advise you to make your choice entirely according to your own taste and to the time you have available. Some of the sweets are both expensive and time-consuming to prepare, but they are so lovely it is worth making the effort for special occasions. Apart from these special ones, you will find many desserts which are economical in money and effort—and delicious too.

Desserts and Puddings

BAKED BREAD PUDDING   SCHEITERHAUFEN

5½ dl (1 pint) milk
2 eggs
240 g (8 oz) stale, crusty white
   bread
75 g (2½ oz) sugar
60 g (2 oz) raisins

60 g (2 oz) sultanas
30 g (1 oz) chopped blanched
   almonds
120 g (4 oz) apple
75 g (2½ oz) butter

Beat the eggs with the milk and pour over the diced bread. Let it stand to absorb the liquid. Transfer a layer of the soaked bread and milk to a greased soufflé dish. Sprinkle some of the sugar, raisins, sultanas, almonds, peeled and sliced apple and flakes of butter over the bread. Follow this with another layer of soaked bread, and continue thus until the ingredients have been used up, finishing with a bread layer. Bake in a moderately hot oven for about 40 minutes. The milk and egg mixture should have set. Serve as soon as possible with single cream.

Note. This pudding can also be steamed in a double saucepan. Cook for approximately 30 minutes until the custard is set.

CURD CHEESE DUMPLINGS   TOPFENKNÖDEL

A very filling dessert which should be preceded by a light course.

240 g (8 oz) curd cheese
150 g (5 oz) butter or margarine
3 eggs, separated
salt

240 g (8 oz) coarse semolina
90 g (3 oz) homemade
*   breadcrumbs, lightly fried in*
*   120 g (4 oz) butter*

Cream the butter with the sieved curd cheese—if the dough is made in an electric blender sieving is not necessary—stir in the yolks, one by one, a pinch of salt and the semolina. Let the mixture stand for a while before folding in the stiffly beaten whites of egg. The dough should be firm enough to handle—if it is too soft, add a little more semolina with the egg whites. Roll lightly between the palms of the hands into dumplings of about 8 cm (3 in) diameter. Lower the dumplings carefully into lightly boiling slightly salted water, and simmer steadily for about 10 minutes, when the dumplings should float on top. Drain. Dredge the hot dumplings in fried breadcrumbs. Sprinkle with sugar. Serve hot.

SNOW DUMPLINGS   SCHNEENOCKERLN

4 whites of egg
165 g (5½ oz) sugar

5 dl (1 pint) milk

Fold the sugar into the stiffly beaten whites of egg. Scoop out portions with a tablespoon, immerse in lightly boiling milk. After letting the milk come to the boil once, lift the dumplings out with a fish slice or with a perforated spoon. Transfer to a dish and when completely cold serve the dumplings with Vanilla Sauce (p. 153)

JAM WHIP   SCHAUMKOCH

150 g (5 oz) caster sugar
150 g (5 oz) jam (apricot is the most suitable, or sieved strawberry or raspberry)

5 whites of egg
60 g (2 oz) chopped blanched almonds

Beat 2 whites of egg with jam and sugar until very thick. Fold in the other 3 whites of egg, beaten very stiffly. Transfer the mixture to a greased soufflé dish. Scatter the chopped almonds over the top and bake in a moderately hot oven for 10 to 15 minutes, until the top is very lightly browned. Serve at once. The jam may be replaced by melted chocolate.

IMPERIAL OMELETTE   KAISERSCHMARRN

This is very popular in chalets high in the mountains as it is in private homes and restaurants in town and country.

5½ dl (1 pint) milk
60 g (2 oz) sugar
2–3 eggs, separated

120 g (4 oz) flour
60 g (2 oz) sultanas
120 g (4 oz) butter

Make a batter from the milk, sugar, yolks of egg and flour. Beat the batter until smooth and frothy. Fold in the sultanas and the stiffly beaten whites of egg. Heat the butter in a pancake pan, pour in the batter and let it brown on one side, turn over and brown the other side. Turn down the heat a little, tear the batter to pieces with a fork and continue cooking and tossing to brown the pieces all over, while the inside stays soft. Transfer to a warm serving dish, sprinkle generously with sugar, keep hot and serve as soon as possible. Serve with Cranberry Sauce or with harvest plums freshly stewed with sugar. Or you could stir in 240 g (½ lb) stoned cherries before folding in the egg whites.

SPONGE OMELETTE   BISKUITOMELETTE

Make a fatless sponge (see basic recipe, p. 124), based on 90 g (3 oz) flour and follow the recipe for Sponge Slices (p. 124). When the sponge is baked, turn it out on to a wooden surface, quickly spread one half with jam or with whipped cream, fold the other half over and sprinkle with caster sugar. Serve hot.

MOOR IN HIS NIGHTIE   MOHR IM HEMD

60 g (2 oz) butter or margarine   *60 g (2 oz) dark grated chocolate*
3 eggs, separated   *90 g (3 oz) caster sugar*
60 g (2 oz) grated, unskinned   *1 dl (4 oz) double cream and a*
almonds   *dessertspoon sugar*

Cream the butter until fluffy and stir in the egg yolks, sugar, almonds and chocolate. Finally fold in the stiffly beaten whites of egg. Transfer the mixture to a buttered and sugared pudding basin, secure the top and steam for 1 hour. Turn out and surround the pudding with a wreath of double cream whipped with sugar. Serve at once after turning out.

POPPYSEED NOODLES   MOHNNUDELN

Boil 480 g (1 lb) of noodles in water until tender. Drain. Douse very quickly under the cold tap. Toss the noodles in 90 g (3 oz) hot butter, stir in 90 g (3 oz) medium-ground poppyseeds and, before serving, sprinkle with 60 g (2 oz) sugar.

Substitute grated walnuts for the poppyseeds to make NUT NOODLES.

CURD CHEESE PANCAKES   TOPFENPALATSCHINKEN

10 pancakes   *75 g (2½ oz) butter or margarine*

60 g (2 oz) granulated sugar   1 dl (4 oz) sour cream
120 g (4 oz) curd cheese   60 g (2 oz) sultanas
2 eggs, separated

Make 10 pancakes in your usual way and keep them hot while you make the filling. Cream the butter with the sugar, stir in the curd cheese, the yolks, sultanas, and half the amount of sour cream. Lastly fold in the stiffly beaten whites. Fill the pancakes with the mixture, arrange the rolled-up pancakes in an ovenproof dish, pour the remainder of the sour cream over the top and put the dish in a hot oven for 5 minutes. Serve as soon as possible.

APPLE PANCAKES   APFELPALATSCHINKEN

Fill the pancakes with apple purée made from peeled, cored apples cooked with sugar. Sprinkle the filled, rolled-up pancakes with sugar before serving.

ORANGE or LEMON PANCAKES
ORANGEN-ODER ZITRONENPALATSCHINKEN

Fill the pancakes with the chopped flesh of peeled oranges or lemons, liberally sprinkled with sugar. Let the filling stand for about 1 hour before needed. Roll up the pancakes and sprinkle with sugar.

PANCAKE SOUFFLÉ   PALATSCHINKENAUFLAUF

10 pancakes   105 g (3½ oz) sugar
120 g (4 oz) grated almonds   2½ dl (½ pint) milk beaten with
90 g (3 oz) sultanas   3 egg yolks

Sprinkle the open pancake with almonds, sultanas and sugar, roll up and cut in half crossways. Transfer to a greased soufflé dish and arrange in layers. Pour the milk and yolks over the top, and bake in a moderately hot oven for ½ hour. Serve as soon as possible.

SEMOLINA PUDDING SAUTÉD GRIESS SCHMARRN

5¼ dl (1 pint) milk	45 g (1½ oz) sugar
120 g (4 oz) coarse semolina	salt
120 g (4 oz) margarine or butter	

Into the boiling milk sprinkle semolina and a pinch of salt. Stir and cook until very thick. Heat the butter in a pancake pan and transfer the semolina mixture, patting it down to cover the bottom of the pan. Lower the heat, cover the pan, and when one side has browned turn over and brown the other side. Tear to pieces with a fork, stir in the sugar, replace the cover on the pan and continue cooking, tossing frequently, until the semolina pieces are golden brown outside but remain soft in the centre. Transfer to a serving dish, sprinkle with sugar and, as soon as possible, serve with freshly stewed plums and sugar, or with a fruit syrup.

Fruit Desserts

APPLES BAKED IN SOUR CREAM RAHMÄPFEL

5 medium size cooking apples	2 eggs, separated
90 g (3 oz) butter or margarine	75 g (2½ oz) ground almonds
60 g (2 oz) sugar	3 tablespoons sour cream

Poach the peeled cored apples in very little water and sugar until they are half-cooked. Cream the sugar and butter, stir in the yolks, one by one, the almonds and the sour cream. Lastly fold in the stiffly beaten whites of egg. Transfer the apples to a greased oven-proof dish, pour the sauce over the top and bake in a moderately hot oven for about 40 minutes, until the mixture has risen and is lightly browned on top. Serve at once.

CARAMEL APPLE PURÉE KARAMEL APFELPUREE

Bake or stew peeled and cored cooking apples, and purée them with sugar. Transfer to a fireproof dish, and sprinkle the purée generously with sugar—it should be completely covered. Place under the hot grill until the sugar has caramelized. Serve cold.

FRESH APPLE JELLY   APFELGELEE

240 g (8 oz) granulated sugar   *1 orange*
480 g (1 lb) apples   *30 g (1 oz) blanched almonds*
1 lemon

Boil the sugar with a little water to the 'Bubble Stage'. (See my General Notes, p. 177.) Grate the peeled cored apples into the syrup. Add the juice of 1 lemon and 1 orange. Simmer until a thick pulp is obtained. Stir in 30 g (1 oz) grated blanched almonds. Rinse a jelly mould or a basin with cold water, dredge with granulated sugar and fill with the cooled pulp. Stand in a cool place and turn out next day. The flavour and consistency of the jelly improve if it is made several days before serving.

APPLE WHIP   APFELCREME

240 g (8 oz) lump sugar   *1 dl (⅛ pint) single cream*
480 g (1 lb) apples

Boil the sugar with half the quantity of water until it makes a thick syrup. Peel, core and slice the apples, and simmer in the syrup until soft. Pulp. When completely cold, whip with some single cream until light and frothy. Serve very cold. Undiluted evaporated milk can be used.

APRICOT DUMPLINGS (POTATO PASTRY)
MARILLENKNÖDEL AUS ERDÄPFELTEIG

480 g (1 lb) potatoes   *480 g (1 lb) apricots*
30 g (1 oz) butter   *1 lump of sugar for each apricot*
120–180 g (4–6 oz) plain flour,   *90 g (3 oz) homemade (dried)*
  as needed   *breadcrumbs, lightly fried in*
1 egg lightly beaten with a drop   *butter*
  of milk   *90 g (3 oz) butter or margarine*

Boil the potatoes, peel and mash. Work the hot potatoes into a dough with the butter, egg, a pinch of salt, and enough flour to make it workable. Knead lightly until smooth. Roll into a sausage of about 7 cm (3 in) diameter and cut into 1 cm (½ in) thick slices. Pat or roll out the slices large enough to cover an apricot. Stone the apricots and replace each stone with a lump of sugar. Envelop each apricot with a cover of dough. The fruit must be completely covered, but at the same time the covering should not be too thick. Lower the dumplings into lightly boiling water to which a little salt has been added, and simmer steadily for about 5 minutes. Lift the dumplings out with a perforated spoon and dredge them with the fried breadcrumbs. Pile on a dish and sprinkle generously with sugar. Although at their best when first cooked, the dumplings can be re-heated. Re-heat over steam or in melted butter in the oven or on top of the cooker.

See also page 129.

Plums can also be used to make PLUM DUMPLINGS (ZWETSCHKEN-KNÖDEL).

FRESH BERRY SALAD   BEERENSALAT

Put equal quantities of prepared red and black currants in a bowl, sprinkle liberally with granulated sugar, shake the bowl to distribute the sugar. Prepare at least 1 hour before serving and keep in a cool place or in the refrigerator. Hulled raspberries and strawberries make a good mixture, too. Blackberries are best served on their own, but the others can be served in any combination.

FRUIT FRITTERS   GEBACKENE FRÜCHTE

Make a thick batter from 2½ dl (½ pint) milk, 180 g (6 oz) flour, 2 eggs and a pinch of salt. Coat 480 g (1 lb) fruit with batter. Use pears and apples, peeled, cored and cut into thick slices; stoned and halved plums and apricots; bananas, halved lengthways and halved again. You can use fruit singly, but a mixture of fruit makes the dish most interesting. Fry the coated fruit in hot fat or oil until golden brown and crisp. Lift out with a fish slice and drain well. Pile on a serving dish, sprinkle generously with sugar, keep hot and serve as soon as possible.

REDCURRANT JELLY RIBISELSULZ

480 g (1 lb) redcurrants
240 g (8 oz) granulated sugar

2½ dl (½ pint) double cream
15 g (½ oz) caster sugar

Sieve the prepared currants. Boil the purée for 6 minutes, counting the time from boiling-point. Stir in the sugar and boil for another 6 minutes, again counting the time from boiling-point. Transfer the jelly to a basin rinsed out with cold water, and let it set. When cold enough, put the bowl in the refrigerator. When the jelly has set firmly turn it out on to a dish and keep very cold until ready to serve. Surround the base of the jelly with double cream whipped with the caster sugar.

Cakes and Gâteaux

ALMOND BREAD MANDELBROT

60 g (2 oz) margarine
150 g (5 oz) vanilla sugar
2 eggs
150 g (5 oz) ground almonds

150 g (5 oz) self-raising flour
30 g (1 oz) blanched halved
   almonds

Beat the margarine with the sugar and eggs until frothy. Stir in the almonds and the flour. Transfer the mixture to a small greased and floured loaf tin, decorate the top with the halved almonds and bake in a moderately hot oven for 35–40 minutes until the bread has risen and the top is browned. Turn out on to a cake rack on a wooden surface and leave at room temperature until cold. When the almond bread is completely cold, cut it into slices to serve.

Desserts

ALMOND CAKE
MANDELTORTE

120 g (4 oz) sugar
4 eggs, separated
120 g (4 oz) ground almonds

30 g (1 oz) homemade
*   breadcrumbs*

Beat the sugar and yolks until frothy. Stir in the almonds and fold in the stiffly beaten whites of egg together with the breadcrumbs. Transfer to a greased and floured cake tin and bake in a moderately hot oven for about 1 hour. The cake should be fully cooked before being removed from the oven, or it will collapse. Allow to cool for a few minutes before removing from the cake tin on to a wooden surface. Let the cake get cold at room temperature.

BISHOP'S BREAD
BISCHOFSBROT

150 g (5 oz) sugar
45 g (1½ oz) blanched almonds,
*   chopped*
30 g (1 oz) raisins, chopped

4 eggs, separated
60 g (2 oz) plain chocolate,
*   chopped*
30 g (1 oz) mixed peel, chopped
120 g (4 oz) self-raising flour

Beat the yolks and sugar until frothy. Stir in the almonds, raisins, chocolate and peel, and fold in the stiffly beaten whites of egg alternately with the flour. Transfer the mixture to a greased and floured loaf tin and bake in a moderate oven for 50 minutes to 1 hour, until the 'bread' has risen, is slightly browned and fully cooked. Cut into slices when completely cold.

CHESTNUT PURÉE
KASTANIENREIS

I would not recommend using tinned chestnut purée as a dessert or in any of my other chestnut recipes.

480 g (1 lb) chestnuts in their
*   shells or*

360 g (12 oz) dried chestnuts
180 g (6 oz) icing sugar

Slit the chestnuts across their round sides with a sharp knife and bake them on a dampened sheet for 10 minutes in a hot oven, until they can be peeled easily. Transfer the chestnuts to a saucepan containing boiling water and boil until very soft. I prefer boiling them unpeeled to retain their full flavour, and this way they take about 20 minutes; half that time if they are peeled. Drain, and put them through a sieve or in an electric blender. Stir the icing sugar into the purée. Beat until smooth.

To serve in the traditional Viennese way, as a dessert, pass the mixture through the back of a coarse grater into a bowl, where it will emerge in the shape of little 'worms'. However, I usually dispense with that additional chore, which also inevitably wastes some of the purée, by lightly piling the purée in a serving dish, and forking it up. Serve cold with 4 oz double cream whipped with 15 g (½ oz) sugar arranged in a wreath around it and with hot or cold chocolate sauce.

Using dried chestnuts is a great economy in labour but it makes the dish more expensive. Soak dried chestnuts overnight before boiling them in the water in which they have been soaked. After this use them like fresh chestnuts.

CHESTNUT CAKE KASTANIENTORTE

240 g (8 oz) chestnuts in their shells or	30 g (1 oz) ground almonds
180 g (6 oz) dried chestnuts	15 g (½ oz) homemade breadcrumbs
150 g (5 oz) caster sugar	1 dl (4 oz) double cream
3 eggs, separated	15 g (½ oz) sugar

Make a Chestnut Purée (p. 116). Beat the sugar with the yolks until frothy, stir with the almonds and the breadcrumbs into the cold purée. Lastly fold in the stiffly beaten whites of egg. Transfer the mixture to a greased and floured cake tin and bake in a moderate oven for about 50 minutes. The cake must be fully cooked before being removed from the oven, or it will collapse. Turn out on to a wooden surface and let it get cold at room temperature. When the cake is completely cold cut it in half and sandwich with the double cream whipped with 15 g (½ oz) sugar. Ice the cake with chocolate icing or serve with cold Chocolate Sauce I (p. 153).

Another version of this cake omits the almonds and the bread-crumbs, and substitutes 105 g (3½ oz) grated plain chocolate and 15 g (½ oz) flour. Stir the chocolate into the purée, and fold in the flour with the beaten egg whites.

CREAM BUNS   INDIANERKRAPFEN

3 eggs, separated	*45 g (1½ oz) caster sugar*
90 g (3 oz) sugar	*1 dl (4 oz) double cream and 60 g*
3 tablespoons water	*(2 oz) sugar*
120 g (4 oz) self-raising flour	*chocolate icing*

Beat the yolks and sugar until frothy. Gradually add the water and flour and finally fold in the stiffly beaten whites into which the caster sugar has been stirred. Transfer the mixture to greased and floured bun tins. Bake in a moderate oven for about 15 minutes. The buns should be firm but not yet coloured. Transfer the buns to a wooden board, cut a slice off each bun and scoop out most of the sponge. When they are completely cold fill them with whipped cream into which sugar has been beaten. Sandwich two buns together and ice with Chocolate Icing (p. 156).

CHOCOLATE CREAM CAKE   SCHOKOLADECREMETORTE

90 g (3 oz) unsalted butter	*180 g (6 oz) melted plain*
180 g (6 oz) sugar	*chocolate*
	4 eggs, separated

Cream the butter and sugar until fluffy. Beat in the egg yolks, one by one, and stir in the melted chocolate. Finally fold in the stiffly beaten whites of egg. Leave half the mixture uncooked and, from the other half, bake two rounds or squares, about 2½ cm (1 in) thick, in a greased and floured Swiss roll tin, or in 18 cm (7 in) sandwich tins. Bake in a moderate oven for 15–20 minutes. When the chocolate 'pastry' is completely cold, sandwich the two halves with the raw cake mixture. Serve with sweetened whipped cream.

CHOCOLATE LAYER CAKE SCHOKOLADEBLÄTTER TORTE

This is a superb dessert, a lot of work and expensive, but well worth it for a special occasion. I have never eaten it anywhere but in Viennese private houses. Our gardener's wife made it at home, and we called it 'Dying Cake' (*Sterbetorte*) because one would leave this world happily after eating it!

45 g (1½ oz) plain flour
120 g (4 oz) unsalted butter or
    margarine
75 g (2½ oz) caster sugar
120 g (4 oz) melted plain
    chocolate

4 eggs

For the filling:
120 g (4 oz) plain chocolate
240 g (8 oz) double cream

Cream the butter and sugar until frothy. Stir in the melted choco-
late and the lightly beaten eggs, one by one. Stir until smooth before adding the next one. Fold in the flour. Spread the mixture very thinly in Swiss roll tins or sandwich tins, so that you will finish with 4 cake layers. Bake in a hot oven for 8 to 10 minutes when the wafers should be crisp or nearly crisp. Transfer them carefully on to a wooden surface, lying singly. While the wafers are getting cold melt the second 120 g (4 oz) of plain chocolate and stir in all but a small quantity of the whipped cream. Sandwich the cold chocolate wafers in layers with the chocolate cream and decorate the top with the remainder of the whipped cream. Cut into slices with a sharp knife or serve the cake in one piece and cut it at table.

CHOCOLATE SAUSAGE   SCHOKOLADEWURST

210 g (7 oz) grated blanched
    almonds
210 g (7 oz) grated plain
    chocolate
1 egg
120 g (4 oz) granulated sugar

45 g (1½ oz) finely chopped
    candied peel
45 g (1½ oz) blanched almonds,
    halved and finely sliced
    lengthways
caster sugar

Mix the grated almonds and chocolate together and stir them

lightly into the egg and sugar which have been beaten until frothy. Add the peel and the sliced almonds. Let the mixture get warm, not hot, over steam—you can stir it lightly. Transfer it to a board covered with caster sugar and roll into a sausage of about 5 cm (2 in) diameter. Let the outside of the sausage take up as much of the caster sugar as possible. Let the sausage rest overnight in a cool place. Cut into thin slices before serving.

PRUNE SAUSAGE   ZWETSCHKENWURST

240 g (8 oz) stewed stoned prunes *120 g (4 oz) chopped walnuts*
210 g (7 oz) granulated sugar *60 g (2 oz) caster sugar*
90 g (3 oz) chopped figs

Boil granulated sugar with a little water until very thick. Stir in the chopped prunes and boil and stir over low heat until a thick mass is obtained. Stir in the chopped figs and walnuts. Transfer to a board covered with caster sugar and roll into a sausage of about 5 cm (2 in) diameter. Let the outside take up as much of the sugar as possible. Leave in a cool place overnight. Cut into thin slices before serving.

SACHER TORTE

150 g (5 oz) margarine
150 g (5 oz) sugar
150 g (5 oz) melted plain chocolate
6 eggs, separated
150 g (5 oz) self-raising flour
about 60 g (2 oz) apricot jam

chocolate icing

For the filling:
60 g (2 oz) melted plain chocolate
45 g (1½ oz) unsalted butter
30 g (1 oz) icing sugar

Cream the margarine and sugar until frothy. Stir in the melted chocolate, add the yolks one by one, beating until smooth before adding the next one. Fold in the stiffly beaten whites of egg alternately with the flour. Transfer the mixture to an 18 cm (7 in) greased and floured cake tin. Make a slight hollow in the centre to ensure even rising. Bake in a moderately hot oven for about 1½ hours.

Inspect after the first hour and if the cake shows any sign of browning lower the heat a little and continue baking until the cake is fully cooked. A thin wooden skewer inserted should come out clean. Turn the cake out on to a cake rack on a wooden surface and let it get cold at room temperature. Cream the filling ingredients together, and when the cake is completely cold cut it in half and spread with the chocolate filling. Spread the top and sides of the cake very thinly with apricot jam. Cover with chocolate icing made from melted chocolate, icing sugar and a little water, or use Chocolate Icing (p. 156) made with boiled sugar. If Sacher Torte is served as a dessert it should be accompanied by whipped cream, served separately.

This mixture may also be used for CHOCOLATE SLICES. Baked in Swiss-roll tins, spread about 2½ cm (1 in) thick, for about 30 minutes in a moderate oven. Cut into strips while it is still warm, then, when completely cold, sandwich the strips with the chocolate filling, and ice with Chocolate Icing (p. 156). (Or sandwich with whipped cream.) Cut again into individual slices when the icing is set.

STAG'S BACK
REHRÜCKEN

75 g (2¼ oz) margarine
165 g (5½ oz) sugar
60 g (2 oz) cooking chocolate
4 eggs, separated
165 g (5¼ oz) unskinned grated almonds

30 g (1 oz) sponge or biscuit crumbs
chocolate icing
30 g (1 oz) blanched almonds, halved and cut lengthways into thin spikes

Cream the melted, but not hot, chocolate with margarine and sugar until frothy. Beat in the yolks, one by one, beating the mixture until smooth before adding the next one. Stir in the grated almonds and fold in the very stiffly beaten egg whites together with the sweet crumbs. The cake should be baked in a long narrow tin with an indentation down the centre of the rounded back—the 'stag's backbone'. Failing this special tin, use a long loaf tin. Transfer the mixture to the greased and floured tin and bake in a moderate oven for about 1 hour until quite firm. Turn out on to a wooden surface and allow to get cold at room temperature. Ice with Chocolate Icing (p. 156). When the icing is hard decorate it all over with the almond sticks standing upright. This represents the larding in a roasted stag's back.

VIENNESE CAKE   WIENER TORTE

150 g (5 oz) margarine
4 eggs, separated
150 g (5 oz) sugar
*60 g (2 oz) melted plain
    chocolate*

*150 g (5 oz) unskinned ground
    almonds*
*120 g (4 oz) Chocolate Cake
    Filling*
*2 dl (8 oz) double cream,
    whipped with 1 oz sugar*

Cream the margarine with the melted, cooled-down chocolate, sugar and yolks of egg until fluffy, and fold in the stiffly beaten whites of egg together with the almonds. Transfer the mixture to an 18 cm (7 in) greased and floured cake tin and bake in a moderate oven for about 1 hour, or until the cake is fully cooked—not before, or it might collapse. Leave in the tin for a few minutes before turning out on to a cake rack on a wooden surface. Allow it to get cold at room temperature. When the cake is completely cold cut it in half and sandwich with Chocolate Cake Filling (p. 155). Cover the cake all over with whipped cream.

SPONGE CAKE   BISKUIT TORTE

3 eggs
3 eggs' weight self-raising flour
2 eggs' weight margarine

2 eggs' weight granulated sugar
1 teaspoon lemon juice

Cream the margarine, sugar and lemon juice until frothy, separate the eggs and stir the yolks one by one into the creamed mixture. Beat until smooth before adding the next one. Alternately fold in the flour and the stiffly beaten whites of egg. Transfer the mixture to a greased and floured 18 cm (7 in) cake tin and bake in a moderately hot oven for about 45 minutes, until the cake is fully cooked. Turn out on to a cake rack on a wooden surface and let it get cold at room temperature. This basic cake can be varied in many ways, or sliced in half and filled with some of my suggested cake-fillings, then iced or decorated with sugar.

CHERRY SPONGE CAKE   KIRSCHEN BISKUITTORTE

Follow the recipe for Sponge Cake (p. 122). Transfer the mixture to a greased and floured 18 cm (7 in) cake tin. Cover the uncooked mixture with 240 g (½ lb) fresh cherries and bake in a moderately hot oven for about 50 minutes, until the cake is fully cooked. The cherries will be embodied in the sponge. Turn out on to a cake rack on a wooden surface, sprinkle with sugar while still hot and let the cake get cold at room temperature.

FRUIT LAYER SPONGE   OBST BISKUITTORTE

Bake a Sponge Cake (p. 122). When the cake is completely cold, slice it into three equal layers. Spread the bottom layer thinly with jam. Cover with raspberries or strawberries crushed with sugar; or grapes; or fresh, skinned sliced peaches; or halved, stoned apricots; or prepared red or black currants sprinkled with sugar; or fresh or tinned pineapple chunks. Place the second layer of sponge on top and spread 2½ cm (1 in) thick with double cream whipped with a little sugar. Spread the third sponge layer with jam, cover with more fruit and place on top of the whipped cream layer. Cover the top of the cake with more whipped cream and decorate with chopped angelica.

SPONGE GUGLHUPF   BISKUIT GUGLHUPF

Make a Sponge Cake mixture (p. 122) but stir in 60 g (2 oz) sultanas before folding in the stiffly beaten whites of egg and the flour. Grease and flour a Guglhupf mould (see Traditional Guglhupf (p. 144)) and line it with blanched almonds halved lengthways. Transfer the cake mixture to the mould. Leave the opening of the funnel free of dough. Bake in a moderately hot oven for about 45 minutes until the Guglhupf has risen, is lightly browned and fully cooked. Turn out on to a cake rack on a wooden surface, sprinkle with caster sugar while hot, and let the cake get cold at room temperature.

MARBLED GUGLHUPF   MARMOR GUGLHUPF

Make a sponge mixture as in the previous recipe. Into half the mixture stir 60 g (2 oz) cocoa, previously beaten until smooth with 2 tablespoons water. Grease, flour and line with almonds a Guglhupf tin, as before. Transfer the mixture, in alternate layers of white and chocolate sponge, to the tin. Bake and turn out as before.

SALZBURG DUMPLINGS   ECHTE SALZBURGER NOCKERLN

75 g (2¼ oz) butter	*30 g (1 oz) flour*
150 g (5 oz) caster sugar	*3½ dl (12 oz) milk*
6 eggs, separated	*sugar for sprinkling*

Cream the butter with sugar and yolks until frothy. Fold in the stiffly beaten whites of egg and the flour. Transfer the mixture to a baking dish into which very hot milk has been poured, and bake for a few minutes in a very hot oven. The sponge should be light brown. Scoop out large portions of the sponge with a tablespoon, pile on a warmed dish, sprinkle with sugar and serve at once.

See also page 129.

SPONGE SLICES   BISKUITSCHNITTEN

This is a basic recipe for fatless sponge.

90 g (3 oz) granulated sugar	*90 g (3 oz) self-raising flour*
3 small or 2 large eggs	

Whisk the sugar and eggs until thick and frothy. Fold in the flour. Spread about 1 cm (½ in) thick on a greased and floured Swiss roll-type tin and bake in the centre of a moderately hot oven for about 10–15 minutes, or until the sponge has risen and is lightly browned. Turn out on to a cake rack on a wooden surface. Sprinkle the sponge generously with caster sugar while hot. Serve cold, cut in slices. Or if you wish to fill the slices, cut the sponge into 10 cm (4 in) wide strips and spread half of them with a cake-filling. Then top them with the other half and sprinkle with icing sugar, or ice them. Finally cut these long strips into slices.

APRICOT SPONGE SLICES   MARILLENSCHNITTEN

Make a fatless sponge based on 90 g (3 oz) flour and follow the recipe for Sponge Slices. While the sponge is baking, stew 250 g (8 oz) halved, stoned apricots with $\frac{1}{2}$ dl (2 oz) water and 60 g (2 oz) lump sugar. Strain, retaining the syrup. Boil the syrup until it jellies (see my General Notes, p. 177). Allow to cool. Cover the baked sponge slices with the cold apricot halves and cover these with the thick jelly. Serve cold.

Or, if the apricots are ripe, you can place the stoned halves on the unbaked sponge, and proceed as for Cherry Sponge Slices below. Sprinkle liberally with sugar while hot, and serve cold.

CHERRY SPONGE SLICES   KIRSCHENBISKUIT

Make a fatless sponge based on 90 g (3 oz) flour. Spread the mixture $2\frac{1}{2}$ cm (1 in) thick, in a Swiss roll-type tin and place about 240 g (8 oz) fresh cherries in close rows on top. Bake in a moderately hot oven for 15–20 minutes, or until the sponge is fully baked and lightly browned. The cherries will be embedded in the sponge. Sprinkle with caster sugar while hot, cut into slices, and serve cold.

POPPYSEED CAKE   MOHNTORTE

120 g (4 oz) margarine
120 g (4 oz) sugar
4 eggs, separated
120 g (4 oz) ground walnuts

120 g (4 oz) ground poppyseeds
45 g (1$\frac{1}{2}$ oz) mixed candied peel,
chopped small

Cream the margarine and sugar until fluffy, stir in the yolks, one by one, beating until smooth before adding the next one. Stir in the ground walnuts and poppyseeds, followed by the finely chopped peel. Lastly fold in the stiffly beaten whites of egg. Transfer the mixture to a greased and floured 18 cm (7 in) cake tin and bake in a moderate oven for about 1 hour. The cake contains no flour and must be fully baked before being removed from the oven or it will collapse. Let it cool in the tin for a few minutes before removing it to a wooden surface. Let the cake get cold at room temperature. Sprinkle with icing sugar.

SAND CAKE   SANDTORTE

240 g (8 oz) margarine   *240 g (8 oz) self-raising flour*
240 g (8 oz) sugar   *jam*
2 eggs, separated   *icing sugar*
1 teaspoon lemon juice

Cream the margarine and sugar until frothy, stir in the lemon juice, and add the yolks, beating them in one by one. Fold in the stiffly beaten whites of egg alternately with the flour. Transfer the mixture to a greased and floured 18 cm (7 in) cake tin and bake in a moderately hot oven for about 40 minutes. Turn out on to a cake rack on a wooden surface and let the cake get cold at room temperature. When completely cold, cut it in half and sandwich with jam or marmalade. Sprinkle liberally with icing sugar on top and score the sugar with a fork in a crisscross pattern.

SEMOLINA CAKE   GRIESSTORTE

4 eggs, separated   *75 g (2½ oz) semolina*
135 g (4½ oz) sugar   *juice and grated rind of 1 lemon*
45 g (1½ oz) ground almonds

Beat the yolks and sugar until frothy. Stir in the almonds, lemon juice and rind and fold in the semolina alternately with the stiffly beaten whites of egg. Transfer to a greased and floured 18 cm (7 in) cake tin and bake in a moderately hot oven for about 40 minutes.

Desserts

WAFER CAKE

This cake can be very quickly made from large round wafers, *Oblaten*, obtainable in delicatessen shops. Handle the wafers carefully, they are very brittle.

Make a pile of 4–6 wafers sandwiched together with thick layers of cake-filling. Pipe or spread the top wafer with double cream whipped with a little sugar. Sprinkle the top with chopped or shredded plain chocolate.

WALNUT CAKE

60 g (2 oz) margarine
180 g (6 oz) caster sugar
3 eggs, separated
60 g (2 oz) cocoa
¼ dl (2 oz) very strong black coffee

60 g (2 oz) ground walnuts
120 g (4 oz) self-raising flour
coffee icing
30 g (1 oz) halved walnuts

Cream the margarine and sugar and beat in the yolks one by one, beating until smooth before adding the next one. Mix the cocoa and coffee into a smooth paste, and beat it in. Beat the mixture until frothy. Fold in the stiffly beaten whites of egg alternately with the flour. Transfer the mixture to a greased and floured 18 cm (7 in) cake tin and bake in a moderately hot oven for about 1 hour, until the cake is fully cooked. Turn out on to a cake rack on a wooden surface and allow the cake to get cold at room temperature. When the cake is completely cold cut it in half, and sandwich with Coffee Cake Filling (p. 155), or with marmalade. Ice with Coffee Icing (p. 156), and decorate with halved walnuts.

Pastries

BASIC CHOUX PASTRY

Use the quantities given in the individual recipes. Bring the milk or water to the boil with the margarine or butter. Lower the heat and beat in the flour, boldly and all at once. Continue beating over low heat until the mixture does not stick to either the pan or the spoon. Transfer to a mixing bowl and stir in the eggs one by one, ensuring that the dough is smooth before adding the next egg. Stir in the sugar.

CHOUX PASTRY PUFFS
BRANDTEIGKRAPFERLN

1 dl (4 oz) water
75 g (2½ oz) margarine
120 g (4 oz) self-raising flour
90 g (30 oz) sugar
3 eggs

1 dl (4 oz) double cream
1 dessertspoon sugar
2½ dl (½ pint) hot Chocolate
  Sauce, optional

Make choux pastry dough from water, margarine, flour, sugar and eggs. Let it rest in a cool place for about ½ hour. Place dessertspoons of the dough in little heaps on a greased and floured baking sheet. Bake in the centre of a moderately hot oven for 15 to 20 minutes, until the puffs have risen and are fully cooked. Do not open the oven door for the first 10 minutes and do not remove the baking sheet for inspection from the oven but have a quick look through the narrowly opened oven door. The puffs collapse at a change of temperature before they are fully cooked. Transfer the fully cooked and lightly browned puffs to a wooden surface and let them cool down at room temperature. When completely cold, make an incision in the centre of each puff and fill with double cream whipped with a dessertspoon sugar. Sprinkle the puffs lightly with icing sugar. If wished, serve with hot Chocolate Sauce (p. 153).

APRICOT OR PLUM DUMPLINGS
(CHOUX PASTRY) zwetschken oder marillenknödel
AUS BRANDTEIG

For the choux pastry:
2½ dl (½ pint) water
30 g (1 oz) margarine

150 g (5 oz) plain flour
2 eggs
pinch of salt

480 g (1 lb) apricots
1 lump sugar for each fruit
90 g (3 oz) homemade
  breadcrumbs

90 g (3 oz) butter or margarine
sugar for sprinkling on the
  dumplings

Make a choux pastry dough, then follow the recipe for Apricot Dumplings made from Potato Pastry (p. 113). Like that recipe, these dumplings can be made with plums.

See also page 114.

SALZBURG DUMPLING SOUFFLÉ

SALZBURGER NOCKERLN AUS BRANDTEIG

For the choux pastry:
1½ dl (¼ pint) milk
45 g (1½ oz) margarine
120 g (4 oz) flour
3 eggs
45 g (1½ oz) sugar

1 dl (4 oz) milk and 1 dl (4 oz)
  water, with a pinch of salt
75 g (2½ oz) unsalted butter
120 g (4 oz) vanilla sugar
2 eggs, separated

Make a choux dough. Scoop out portions of the mixture with a dessertspoon and immerse them in the nearly boiling milk and water. The liquid should be 'trembling'. Remove from the heat and let the dumplings 'draw' for 10 minutes, like making tea. Drain. Meanwhile, cream the butter, vanilla sugar and egg yolks until frothy and fold in the stiffly beaten whites of egg and the drained cold dumplings. Transfer the mixture to a greased soufflé dish and bake in a hot oven for 40 minutes. Sprinkle with sugar and serve at once.

See also page 124.

CHOUX PASTRY FRITTERS

SPRITZKRAPFEN

For the choux pastry:
1½ dl (¼ pint) water
60 g (2 oz) margarine
75 g (2½ oz) flour

2 eggs
15 g (½ oz) sugar
fat or oil for frying
sugar for sprinkling

Make a choux dough and pipe or spoon narrow portions, about

E

10 cm (4 in) long like little éclairs, into hot fat and fry golden brown and crisp. Lift out with a fish slice and drain off the fat. Pile on a dish, sprinkle liberally with sugar and serve as soon as possible.

CHOUX PASTRY OMELETTE   BRANDTEIGOMELETTE

For the choux pastry:
30 g (1 oz) margarine
2½ dl (½ pint) milk
30 g (1 oz) flour
3 eggs
1 teaspoon granulated sugar

240 g (½ lb) peeled, cored and
    sliced cooking apples or pears
    cooked with 240 g (½ lb) sugar
    and a drop of water
about 2½ dl (½ pint) chocolate
    sauce

Make a choux dough and spread out the mixture on a large, greased ovenproof plate or shallow dish. Bake in the centre of a hot oven for 30–40 minutes, until the omelette has fully risen and is light brown in colour. Do not open the oven door for the first 10 minutes. When at a later stage you want to inspect the omelette, open the door as narrowly as possible and do not remove the omelette from the heat until it is fully cooked. Lift the omelette out on to a wooden surface, fill half the omelette with the stewed apples or pears, fold the other half over, sprinkle with sugar and serve with Chocolate Sauce (p. 153).

CHOUX PASTRY SOUFFLÉ   BRANDTEIGAUFLAUF

For the choux pastry:
4 dl (¾ pint) milk
60 g (2 oz) margarine
90 g (3 oz) flour
60 g (2 oz) sugar

4 eggs, separated
about 2½ dl (½ pint) raspberry or
    blackcurrant syrup diluted with
    a little water

Make a choux pastry dough, using 4 egg yolks. Fold in the stiffly beaten whites of egg. Transfer the mixture to a greased soufflé dish, about 1 l (2 pints) capacity, and bake in a moderate oven for 50 minutes to 1 hour until the soufflé has risen and is lightly browned on top. Sprinkle with sugar and serve at once with a cold fruit syrup.

CURD CHEESE PASTRY TURNOVERS

120 g (4 oz) curd cheese   *120 g (4 oz) plain flour*
120 g (4 oz) butter or margarine *marmalade or jam*

Work curd cheese, butter and flour into a dough. Let it rest in a cool place for about ½ hour before rolling out about 5 mm (¼ in) thick. Cut into 10 cm (4 in) squares, put jam or marmalade in the centre of each square, fold into triangles, and secure the edges with a dampened fork. Brush over with cold water and bake on a greased baking sheet, on the centre shelf of a hot oven, for about 15 minutes, until the pastry is firm and lightly browned. Lift out, sprinkle generously with caster sugar, and serve hot or cold.

APPLE TURNOVER WITH CURD CHEESE PASTRY

450 (15 oz) curd cheese pastry   *90 g (3 oz) sugar*
240 g (½ lb) cooking apples   *60 g (2 oz) sultanas*

Make curd cheese pastry following the method for Curd Cheese Pastry Turnovers, but using 150 g (5 oz) proportions. Roll out the pastry about 5 mm (¼ in) thick into a rectangle. Fill half the pastry, starting from a broad side, with peeled, sliced apples. Sprinkle with sugar and sultanas. Fold the empty flap of pastry over. Dampen the edges and press down with a fork. Brush over with water and bake on a greased baking sheet in a moderately hot oven for 30–40 minutes, until the pastry is firm and lightly browned. Transfer carefully to a wooden surface (preferably on a cake rack to avoid a cold surface), sprinkle with caster sugar. Serve hot or cold.

Use stoned, sliced apricots or plums instead of apples for APRICOT or PLUM TURNOVER, use rhubarb cut into short lengths for RHUBARB TURNOVER.

LINZER TORTE

105 g (3½ oz) plain flour   *105 g (3½ oz) sugar*

210 g (7 oz) margarine
210 g (7 oz) ground almonds
juice and grated rind of 1 lemon
1 dessertspoon cocoa

¼ teaspoon each mixed spice,
* cinnamon, ginger*
1 egg yolk
about 90 g (3 oz) redcurrant or
* raspberry jam*

Work flour, sugar, margarine, almonds, cocoa, peel, spices, lemon juice and egg yolk into a dough. Knead thoroughly. Let the dough rest for ½ hour in a cool place. Roll out about 5 mm (¼ in) thick to fit an 18 cm (7 in) cake tin. Reserve enough of the dough to roll a 1 cm (½ in) diameter sausage to go round the base as well as thinner rolls for a criss-cross lattice over the top. Press the thick roll lightly to the sides of the tin right round the base. Spread the base with jam and cover with a lattice of thin pastry rolls. Brush the pastry with white of egg, or with cold water, and bake in a moderate oven on a low shelf for about 1 hour, until the pastry feels firm to the touch. Sprinkle with caster sugar and let the cake cool a little before turning out of the tin. Serve cold.

APPLES IN DRESSING-GOWNS   ÄPFEL IM SCHLAFROCK

Peel, core but keep whole 480 g (1 lb) of medium-sized apples. Poach in a little water to which sugar has been added. The apples must stay whole. Drain. Roll out 480 g (1 lb) packet of puff pastry about 5 mm (¼ in) thick and cut into 10 cm (4 in) squares. Put an apple in the centre of each square and fill the hollow centres of the apples with a little jam or marmalade. Envelop the apples with pastry by joining the four corners of each square on top of the apple. Fasten the 'dressing-gown tops' with pins cut from thinly sliced blanched almonds. Transfer the apples to a damp baking sheet, brush the pastry over with a lightly beaten egg or with water, and bake in a moderately hot oven on a low shelf for 30–40 minutes, until the pastry is puffed and lightly browned. Remove from the baking sheet, sprinkle with caster sugar and serve with single cream. I think these apples are nicest when served hot, but they can be served cold.

APPLE TURNOVER WITH PUFF PASTRY
APFELSTRUDEL AUS BLÄTTERTEIG

480 g (1 lb) packet of puff pastry   *90 g (3 oz) sugar*
240 g (½ lb) apples   *60 g (2 oz) sultanas*

Roll out puff pastry about 5 mm (¼ in) thick into an oblong shape. Cover the centre of the oblong with peeled sliced apples, and sprinkle with sugar and sultanas. Fold the pastry from all sides into the middle and secure the joins with white of egg or cold water. Brush over the pastry with white of egg or cold water. Bake on a dampened baking sheet in a moderately hot oven for 30 minutes until the pastry is puffed and lightly browned. Sprinkle with caster sugar and serve hot or cold with whipped or single cream.

PUFF PASTRY CAKE
BLÄTTERTEIGTORTE

Roll out 480 g (1 lb) packet of puff pastry about 5 mm (¼ in) thick and cut into 3 equal rounds, using an 18 cm (7 in) cake tin or a plate as a guide. Brush the rounds with beaten egg and bake in a hot oven for 10–15 minutes. When the pastry rounds are cold, place the 2 lower ones on top of one another, each spread thickly with Vanilla Cake Filling (p. 154). Place the third round on top, spread it with whipped cream and pipe an edge of whipped cream around. Decorate the whipped cream to taste—with chocolate drops, or angelica cut into small pieces, or with small, fresh strawberries or raspberries.

PUFF PASTRY FANCIES
KAPRIZEN

Roll out 480 g (1 lb) packet of puff pastry about 5 mm (¼ in) thick. Cut a number of slices 10 cm (4 in) wide, then cut some 1 cm (½ in) strips the same length, brush the long edges of the slices with cold water and lightly press down a 1 cm (½ in) strip each side. Brush over with cold water and bake on a dampened baking sheet in a hot oven for 10–15 minutes. When the pastry is cold, spread the hollow part of the strips with jam, cover this with whipped cream, to which a little sugar has been added. Cut into convenient lengths with a sharp knife.

For SWEET VOL-AU-VENT, follow the recipe for Savoury Vol-au-Vent (p. 33). Fill the cold pastry cases with double cream, whipped with a little sugar, and sprinkle the pastry cases with icing sugar.

CREAM HORNS   BLÄTTERTEIG SKARNITZELN

To make this confection you need those tin horns available in hardware stores.

Roll out 240 g (8 oz) packet of puff pastry very thin, no more than 2 mm ($\frac{1}{8}$ in) thick, and cut into strips, $2\frac{1}{2}$ cm (1 in) wide. Brush with cold water and wind round the dampened tins. Begin working at the pointed end, cover the surface completely, overlapping as little as possible. Brush the pastry with white of egg or water, transfer the horns to a dampened baking sheet and bake in a hot oven until the pastry is lightly browned and can be easily slid off the tins. If the inside of the pastry horns is not completely baked, return the horns to the oven for a few minutes at a reduced heat. Let the horns get cold, then fill with double cream whipped with a little sugar. Wild strawberries or small cultivated strawberries can be placed on top of the whipped cream. Sprinkle the pastry with icing sugar.

BASIC SHORTBREAD PASTRY   MÜRBER TEIG

I decided a long time ago to disregard all the slightly differing recipes for shortbread pastry and to use one single basic recipe given to me by my mother.

3 parts plain flour to 2 parts fat to 1 part sugar. Thus, 270 g (9 oz) plain flour, 180 g (6 oz) margarine or butter and 90 g (3 oz) caster sugar, with a little grated lemon rind. I shall refer to these quantities as '270 g (9 oz) pastry' in any recipe. Knead thoroughly into a smooth dough and let it rest in a cool place for $\frac{1}{2}$ hour before using as required. (If you despair of handling it, you can cheat by adding an egg yolk.)

SHORTBREAD CASE　　　　　MÜRBE TORTENHÜLLE

Line a 18 cm (7 in) cake tin with 270 g (9 oz) shortbread pastry rolled out about 5 mm ($\frac{1}{4}$ in) thick, and about 2$\frac{1}{2}$ cm (1 in) larger than the tin. Press the surplus pastry lightly up the sides of the tin. Bake blind in a moderate oven until the pastry is half-cooked— about 15 minutes—then remove the coverings and bake the case fully—about another 15–25 minutes.

SHORTBREAD FRUIT TART　　　MÜRBER OBSTKUCHEN

Bake a 270 g (9 oz) Shortbread Case as above. Let the turned-out pastry case get completely cold. Spread the base thinly with jam and cover with several layers of prepared red or black currants liberally sprinkled with sugar. Or fill the pastry case with raspberries or strawberries sprinkled with sugar and covered with whipped double cream; or with fresh, peeled and sliced peaches or apricots; or with cold, well-drained stewed fruit or rhubarb.

CHEESE CAKE　　　　　　　TOPFENTORTE

270 g (9 oz) shortbread pastry	*grated rind of $\frac{1}{2}$ lemon*
240 g (8 oz) curd cheese	*75 g (2$\frac{1}{2}$ oz) sugar*
2 eggs, separated	*45 g (1$\frac{1}{2}$ oz) flour*
2$\frac{1}{4}$ dl ($\frac{1}{2}$ pint) milk	*60 g (2 oz) sultanas*

Roll out the pastry about 1 cm ($\frac{1}{2}$ in) thick to fit an 18 cm (7 in) cake tin. Reserve enough pastry to make a roll about 2$\frac{1}{2}$ cm (1 in) thick and long enough to go round the base of the cake. Press the roll lightly against the sides of the tin to make a pastry case. Bake the pastry blind in a moderate oven until half-baked. Meanwhile make the filling. Sieve the curd cheese (unless you use an electric blender, when sieving is not necessary). Cream the cheese with the egg yolks and milk and mix until smooth. Stir in the rind and the sugar and fold in the stiffly beaten whites of egg with the flour. Transfer the filling to the half-baked case, scatter sultanas over the top and bake in a slow oven until the filling has set—about 35–40 minutes.

The filling must not rise. Allow the cheese cake to cool before removing it from the tin. Serve hot or cold.

SHORTBREAD CUSTARD TART MÜRBER CREMEKUCHEN

Half-bake blind a Shortbread Case (p. 135) in an 18 cm (7 in) tin. Beat together 1 dl (4 oz) single cream, 1 egg and 30 g (1 oz) vanilla sugar. Transfer the mixture to the pastry case in the cake tin and return to the moderate oven for about 20 minutes, until the custard has set. Serve cold.

POPPYSEED TART   MOHNKUCHEN

270 g (9 oz) shortbread pastry   *60 g (2 oz) chopped mixed peel*
2 eggs, separated   *90 g (3 oz) ground poppyseeds*
90 g (3 oz) sugar   *60 g (2 oz) sultanas*

Bake the shortbread pastry blind in an 18 cm (7 in) tin, to form a case as in Cheese Cake (p. 135). Remove when half-baked. Meanwhile make the filling. Beat the sugar with the yolks until frothy, stir in the peel, the poppyseeds and the sultanas. Lastly fold in the stiffly beaten whites of egg. Transfer the mixture to the half-baked pastry case in the cake tin and return to a moderate oven until the cake is fully baked and the filling has set—about 20 minutes. Allow to cool down before removing from the tin. Serve cold.

REDCURRANT TART   RIBISELKUCHEN

270 g (9 oz) shortbread pastry   *1 dessertspoon jam or jelly,*
240 g (8 oz) prepared redcurrants   *without pips*
240 g (8 oz) sugar   *¼ dl (2 oz) double cream, optional*

Roll out the pastry to fit an 18 cm (7 in) cake tin. Reserve enough pastry to make a roll of about 1 cm (½ in) diameter, long enough to go round the base of the tart. Press the roll lightly against the sides of the tin, to make a pastry case. Bake blind, and let the fully baked pastry case get cool before removing from the tin. Spread the bottom of the pastry case with the jam or jelly, cover with 60 g (2 oz) prepared redcurrants. Sprinkle with sugar. Boil the remainder of the redcurrants fast with the sugar and a very little water until they form a thick jelly, about 5 or 10 minutes. Transfer to a chilled bowl, and when cold enough, to the refrigerator. When the jelly *starts* setting, pour it evenly over the redcurrants in the pastry case. Return to the refrigerator for quick setting. The top of the jelly can be piped with whipped cream. (This can safely be made the day before.)

REDCURRANT MERINGUE TART

RIBISEL BAISERKUCHEN

270 g (9 oz) shortbread pastry	For the meringue:
240 g (8 oz) redcurrants	*3 whites of egg*
120 g (4 oz) sugar	*75 g (2½ oz) granulated sugar*
1 dl (4 oz) water	

Bake a Shortbread Case (p. 135) in an 18 cm (7 in) tin. While the pastry is baking boil the stripped currants with sugar and water until a thick jelly is obtained. (See my General Notes, p. 177.) Let the jelly cool before transferring it to the pastry case in the cake tin. Fold the 75 g (2½ oz) sugar into the very stiffly beaten whites of egg, and spread the meringue mixture over the redcurrant jelly. Return the cake to a moderate oven until the meringue has set and is lightly coloured.

SHORTBREAD PASTRY CUPS   MÜRBE SCHÜSSERLN

Roll out 270 g (9 oz) shortbread pastry about 5 mm (¼ in) thick and cut into rounds of about 5 cm (2 in) diameter, to fit bun tins. Line the bun tins with pastry, press down the edges with a fork and bake blind in a moderate oven until the pastry is half-cooked. Remove the coverings and bake for another 15 minutes, or until the pastry is fully cooked. Let the pastry cool down a little before carefully removing the cups from the tin, on to a wooden surface. Fill the cups with jam or marmalade, or as suggested in the recipes for Redcurrant Tart (p. 136), Shortbread Fruit Tart (p. 135) or Custard

Tart (p. 136). If the cups are to be filled with custard they should only be half-baked before the custard mixture is added.

SHORTBREAD PASTRY TARTLETS

PFIRSICH TORTELETTEN

Make 270 g (9 oz) shortbread pastry and roll out about 5 mm (¼ in) thick. Cut into 7 cm (3 in) rounds reserving enough pastry to sur-round each tartlet with a pastry 'sausage' of about 1 cm (½ in) dia-meter. Damp the underside of the pastry sausage and press a circle lightly round each tartlet. Bake the tartlets blind, and remove coverings half-way through. Spread the fully baked tartlets thinly with jam and place half a fresh peeled peach on each—you can put a blob of cream in the cavity of each peach. Or put fresh raspberries or strawberries, sprinkled with sugar, into the tartlets. Serve cold.

SHORTBREAD STRUDEL

MÜRBER STRUDEL

Roll out 270 g (9 oz) shortbread pastry about 5 mm (¼ in) thick into an oblong. Cover half of the pastry, starting at one of the long sides, with 240 g (8 oz) peeled, cored and sliced apples (or with scraped rhubarb cut into short lengths, or any other suitable fresh fruit). Sprinkle the apple with 180 g (6 oz) sugar and 60 g (2 oz) sultanas (the rhubarb only with 240 g (8 oz) sugar). Roll up the pastry start-ing from the long filled side. Dampen all edges and press down with a fork. Bake on a damp baking sheet in a moderately hot oven for about 35 minutes, until the pastry is firm to the touch and very lightly browned. Sprinkle with caster sugar. Serve hot or cold, with single or double cream served separately.

BASIC STRUDEL DOUGH

STRUDELTEIG

I offer this recipe for any cook who wants to make her own strudel dough. It is a lengthy process which requires, among other things, a large table covered with a cloth, on which to pull out the dough. Of course, the best strudels are made from homemade dough and most Viennese cooks would not dream of using anything else, but I must confess that I often take the easy way out by using bought puff pastry rolled wafer thin. I can also recommend the ready made strudel leaves available in many delicatessen shops, but they are expensive.

240 g (8 oz) plain flour
1 egg
60 g (2 oz) melted butter, or oil

about 1½ dl (¼ pint) lukewarm
water
pinch of salt

Make a hollow in the centre of the flour in a mixing bowl and pour into it the egg beaten with most of the water, a pinch of salt and 30 g (1 oz) melted butter or oil. Stir with a tableknife or with an electric mixer. Add more water if the dough is too stiff to be kneaded. Knead on a floured board until smooth. Leave the dough on the floured board, cover it with a slightly warmed bowl, and allow to rest for ½ hour. Spread a cotton tablecloth on a fairly large table, dust with flour and roll out the dough with a floured rolling-pin as thin as possible. Brush the dough lightly with oil or melted butter and pull it out by hand, starting from the edges, until the dough is semi-transparent. Take care not to tear it. Cut off the thick edges— they can be dried, grated, and used as pasta in soup. The dough can now be used in any appropriate recipe.

APPLE STRUDEL

APFELSTRUDEL

240 g (8 oz) strudel dough
240 g (½ lb) cooking apples
90 g (3 oz) butter or margarine
90 g (3 oz) homemade
  breadcrumbs

90 g (3 oz) granulated sugar
60 g (2 oz) sultanas
30 g (1 oz) butter, melted

Gas Mark 6

Roll out the pastry, so thin as to be transparent, into an oblong shape. Sprinkle two-thirds of the oblong with breadcrumbs lightly fried in the butter or margarine. Cover the breadcrumbs with the peeled, cored, thinly sliced apples. Sprinkle with sugar and sultanas. Sprinkle the remaining third of the dough with melted margarine or butter. Roll up the strudel starting at the filled edge. Seal all edges with a finger dipped in cold water. Transfer the strudel to a greased baking tin and brush the pastry with the melted butter. Bake in a moderately hot oven for 30–35 minutes, until the pastry is firm and nicely browned. Transfer to a serving dish, sprinkle thickly with caster sugar and serve hot or cold. I think the strudel tastes best when served hot soon after baking, with whipped cream or single cream in a separate bowl.

RHUBARB or PLUM or CHERRY or MORELLO CHERRY or GOOSEBERRY or APRICOT STRUDEL

RHABARBER—PFLAUMEN—KIRSCHEN—WEICHSEL—MARILLEN
—ODER STACHELBEER—STRUDEL

Follow the recipe for Apple Strudel (p. 139), treating the various fruit and the rhubarb as follows:

Peel the rhubarb, unless very young, and cut into short lengths. Stone cherries and morello cherries. Stone and halve plums. Stone, halve and, if at all unripe, slice, apricots. Top and tail gooseberries. Rhubarb and gooseberries will need some extra sugar.

CURD CHEESE STRUDEL   TOPFENSTRUDEL

240 g (8 oz) strudel dough   *½ dl (2 oz) sour cream*
60 g (2 oz) butter or margarine   *grated peel of ½ lemon*
60 g (2 oz) sugar   *60 g (2 oz) sultanas*
2 eggs, separated   *30 g (1 oz) butter, melted*
120 g (4 oz) curd cheese   *30 g (1 oz) caster sugar*

Roll out the dough, so thin as to be transparent, into an oblong shape. Make the filling: cream the butter with the sugar, stir in the yolks, sieved curd cheese, lemon rind and sour cream. (If you make the filling in an electric blender the curd cheese need not be sieved.) Lastly, fold in the stiffly beaten whites of egg. Starting at one of the long sides, fill two-thirds of the oblong with the mixture and sprinkle with the sultanas. Roll up the strudel starting from the filled end. Seal all the edges with a finger dipped in cold water. Brush the top with melted butter and bake on a greased baking sheet in a moderately hot oven for about 30–35 minutes, until the pastry is firm and nicely browned. Cut the strudel into portions, transfer them to a serving dish and sprinkle with caster sugar. Serve hot with Vanilla Sauce (p. 153).

POPPYSEED STRUDEL

240 g (8 oz) strudel dough
150 g (5 oz) poppyseeds, ground medium fine
120 g (4 oz) butter or margarine
90 g (3 oz) sugar

3 eggs, separated
juice and grated rind of ½ lemon
1 dessertspoon warmed honey
caster sugar

Cream the butter with the sugar and stir in the poppyseeds, egg yolks, lemon juice and rind, and honey. Lastly fold in the stiffly beaten egg whites. Fill two-thirds of the very thinly rolled-out pastry oblong, starting at a long edge, with the mixture. Roll up the strudel, beginning at the filled long side. Seal all the edges with a finger dipped into cold water. Brush the pastry with melted butter. Transfer to a greased baking sheet and bake in a moderately hot oven for about 30–35 minutes, until the pastry is firm and nicely browned. Cut into portions, transfer to a serving dish and sprinkle with caster sugar. Serve either hot or cold, though I prefer it hot.

VIENNESE TURNOVERS

150 g (5 oz) plain flour
90 g (3 oz) butter or margarine
60 g (2 oz) caster sugar
2 egg yolks

1 tablespoon sour cream
drained, freshly stewed or tinned fruit

Work flour, butter, sugar and yolks into a dough. Work in enough sour cream to make the dough pliable. Rest in a cool place for about ½ hour before rolling out about 5 mm (¼ in) thick. Cut into 10 cm (4 in) squares. Place some fruit in the centre of each square, fold into triangles, dampen the edges and press them down with a fork. Brush over with white of egg or water, and bake on an ungreased baking sheet in a moderately hot oven for about 30 minutes, until the pastry is firm and lightly browned. Lift out, sprinkle with caster sugar and serve hot or cold.

BASIC YEAST DOUGH GERMTEIG

Some general notes that apply to all the yeast recipes.

Before starting to make a yeast dough, weigh and measure the ingredients as given in the recipe and leave them at room temperature at least one hour in advance. To prove the yeast, break it up and stir it into a smooth paste with a little flour, sugar and milk, which can all be taken from the weighed ingredients. The yeast mixture should have the consistency of a pancake batter. Put it to rise in a warm place at no more than 80° F, 27° C. If the temperature is too high, the yeast germs will be destroyed and the mixture will not rise. If the temperature is not high enough, it will not rise either. If, in spite of the right conditions, the yeast does not rise, it is probably too old and should be discarded. Use dried yeast according to the instructions on the packet. In a few recipes containing fresh yeast there is no need to prove it first. When the proving mixture has risen to twice its volume use it as instructed in the recipe. Most yeast doughs must be beaten until they form large bubbles. If this is done by hand with a wooden spoon, the work is made much easier by beating the dough in manageable portions, rather than all at once. If you have an electric mixer with a yeast hook this is, of course, the easiest way of all. Most recipes ask for the yeast dough to rise for at least one hour before being transferred to the baking tin, and usually for another period of rising in the tin. The result is very rewarding, but it means that yeast dough cannot be made in a hurry. When the dough is fully baked a wooden probe inserted in the centre should come out clean. The baked cake should be turned out at once on to a cake rack on a wooden surface to cool at room temperature.

HOT YEAST BUNS DAMPFNUDELN

30 g (1 oz) fresh yeast
180 g (6 oz) plain flour

1 dl (4 oz) milk, as needed
30 g (1 oz) granulated sugar

60 g (2 oz) margarine
2 egg yolks
pinch of salt

75 g (2½ oz) butter
2 tablespoons milk
Vanilla Sauce

Let the weighed flour stand in a mixing bowl, at room temperature, for ½ hour. Prove the yeast. Stir together the yolks, the remainder of the 1 dl (4 oz) milk, the melted margarine, the risen yeast mixture, the flour and a pinch of salt, to form a stiff dough. Beat until the dough forms large bubbles, and leaves the spoon freely. Allow to rise in a warm place for about 1 hour. Roll the dough on a floured board into a sausage of about 4 cm (1½ in) diameter. Cut into 5 mm (¼ in) slices, dip them into the melted butter and transfer to a baking tin containing ½ dl (⅛ pint) warm milk. Let the buns rise to double their size before baking them in a hot oven for 15–20 minutes, or until they are light brown. Serve hot with Vanilla Sauce (p. 153).

CRUMBLE SLICES   STREUSSELKUCHEN

30 g (1 oz) fresh yeast
150 g (5 oz) plain flour
¼ dl (2 oz) milk
2 egg yolks
30 g (1 oz) margarine
15 g (½ oz) granulated sugar

For the crumble:
75 g (2½ oz) plain flour
45 g (1½ oz) sugar
30 g (1 oz) ground almonds
grated rind of ¼ lemon
30 g (1 oz) butter
¼ teaspoon cinnamon

Prove the yeast. Beat together the proved yeast, flour, milk, egg yolks, melted margarine and sugar. Beat until the dough forms large bubbles, and leave it to rise. Meanwhile make the crumble by stirring together the flour, ground almonds, lemon rind, sugar and cinnamon. Let the melted butter drip in and rub all the ingredients together to obtain a coarse mixture. Spread the dough about 1 cm (½ in) thick on a greased baking sheet. Let it rise again for ½ hour. Sprinkle the crumble mixture evenly over the risen dough and bake in a moderately hot oven for about 40 minutes. Serve cold.

TRADITIONAL GUGLHUPF   GERMGUGLHUPF

Although the *Guglhupf* is as much a symbol of Vienna as *Sacher Torte*, *Apfelstrudel*, *Wiener Schnitzel* and *Backhendl* perhaps I should describe the appearance of this cake for those cooks who have never seen it. The traditional Guglhupf is made of a yeast dough—for which the recipe follows below—but as all yeast pastry takes a long time to prepare and bake, a sponge mixture is often substituted. (See separate recipe.) To make a Guglhupf you need a special fluted baking mould. Mine is a copper one, an heirloom from my great-grandmother. At the bottom it has a 20 cm (8½ in) diameter, followed by a 5 cm (2 in) straight rim and tapering in the fluted mould to a 14 cm (5½ in) diameter top. This top has a 2½ cm (1 in) opening where the funnel emerges. The whole thing looks like a hillock. My tin is just right for the quantities given in the following and in the Sponge Guglhupf recipes. The yeast recipe goes stale within a day or two, as bread does. It is particularly delicious accompanied by coffee, and for a real luxury make a yeast Guglhupf on Saturday and serve it for Sunday breakfast, when the slices are often spread with butter.

30 g (1 oz) fresh yeast	about 4 dl (¾ pint) of milk, as
150 g (5 oz) margarine	needed
105 g (3½ oz) granulated sugar	30 g (1 oz) split blanched
3 eggs	almonds
grated rind of 1 lemon	margarine, flour, for the
90 g (3 oz) sultanas	Guglhupf tin
450 g (15 oz) plain flour	

Prove the yeast. Cream the margarine and sugar until frothy. Stir in the eggs, one by one, beating until smooth before adding the next one. Follow this by stirring in the proved yeast mixture. grated rind, sultanas and a pinch of salt. Lastly add the flour and enough milk to make a stiff but workable dough. Beat the dough until it forms bubbles, then transfer it to a Guglhupf tin which has been greased, floured and lined with blanched almonds. Press very firmly, or the almonds will slide off. The opening of the funnel of the tin must be kept free of dough. Let the dough rise to double its height before baking the Guglhupf in a moderately hot oven for about 1 hour, until the top is lightly browned and a wooden probe inserted in the cake comes out clean. Turn out at once on to a cake rack on a wooden surface, sprinkle with caster sugar and allow to get cold at room temperature.

FRIED MICE
GEBACKENE MÄUSE

15 g (½ oz) fresh yeast
1 dl (4 oz) lukewarm milk, as needed
30 g (1 oz) granulated sugar
180 g (6 oz) plain flour
pinch of salt

2 egg yolks
60 g (2 oz) melted margarine
30 g (1 oz) sultanas
240 g (8 oz) fat or oil for frying
fruit syrup to serve

Put the weighed flour in a mixing bowl for about 1 hour before starting to cook. Prove the yeast. Stir together the sugar, yolks, proved yeast mixture, melted margarine, flour, pinch of salt and enough of the lukewarm milk to make a firm, but not stiff, dough. Beat the dough until it forms bubbles and does not stick to the spoon. Stir in the sultanas. Let the dough rise for 1 hour in a warm place. With a tablespoon first dipped into the fat, heated in a deep strong pan, cut out portions of the dough and fry them golden brown in the hot fat. Lift out with a fish slice and let surplus fat drip back. Pile on a serving dish, sprinkle liberally with caster sugar, keep hot until ready to serve, as soon as possible, with fruit syrup.

NUT CRESCENTS
GEFÜLLTE GERMKIPFELN

15 g (½ oz) fresh yeast
½ dl (2 oz) milk
45 g (1½ oz) granulated sugar
2 egg yolks
1 egg
270 g (9 oz) plain flour
180 g (6 oz) margarine

For the filling:
270 g (9 oz) ground walnuts
1 dl (4 oz) hot milk
150 g (5 oz) granulated sugar
30 g (1 oz) finely chopped mixed candied peel
1 teaspoon rum or brandy, optional

Prove the yeast. Rub in the flour with the margarine, stir in the yolks, the sugar and the whole egg—but reserving a little of the egg for brushing over the pastry. Stir in the proved yeast and the remainder of the milk. Knead into a smooth dough and leave it to rise. Mix the filling ingredients together. Roll out the dough to the thickness of the blade of a knife, cut into 10 cm (4 in) squares, put a tablespoon of the cold filling in the centre of each square, fold the pastry into triangles and bend into crescents. Allow to rise again for ½ hour. Brush over with the remainder of the egg, transfer the crescents to a greased baking sheet and bake in a hot oven for 30 minutes, until the pastry is lightly browned. Transfer the baked crescents to a wooden surface. Serve cold. The crescents may also be filled with jam, or with the poppyseed filling suggested in Poppyseed Strudel (p. 141).

SAVARIN   GERMREIFEN

30 g (1 oz) fresh yeast	pinch of salt
75 g (2¼ oz) margarine	½ dl (2 oz) water
15 g (½ oz) granulated sugar	60 g (2 oz) lump sugar
150 g (5 oz) plain flour	rind of 1 lemon
3 eggs	rum or brandy
1dl (4 oz) milk	

Prove the yeast. Cream the margarine and sugar, stir in the eggs, one by one, the proved yeast mixture, flour, milk and a pinch of salt. Beat the dough until it forms big bubbles. Transfer to a greased and floured 18 cm (7 in) circular tube cake tin. Let the dough rise in the tin before baking it in a moderately hot oven for about 30 minutes until the dough is firm and lightly browned. Turn out at once on to a cake rack on a wooden surface and allow to cool at room temperature. While the cake is baking, boil ½ dl (2 oz) water with 60 g (2 oz) lump sugar and some lemon rind until the syrup is very thick. Discard the rind. Stir in a little rum or brandy if available. Pour this mixture over the still warm ring on a serving dish. When cold, pile the centre of the ring with sliced fresh oranges or peaches, sprinkled with sugar, or with tinned peaches. Instead of pouring the sugar sauce over the hot ring, the cold savarin can be decorated with whipped cream.

Desserts

Creams and Ices

ICED RICE

KALTER REIS

180 g (6 oz) rice
juice of 1 orange
120 g (4 oz) lump sugar
1 dl (4 oz) water

For the custard:
2 dl (8 oz) single cream
5 egg yolks
60 g (2 oz) vanilla sugar
30 g (1 oz) gelatine
2 dl (8 oz) double cream

Boil the rice in water until tender. Drain. Boil the lump sugar in the water to a thick syrup. Stir in the orange juice. Set aside to get cold. Beat the single cream, the yolks and the vanilla sugar over steam to a thick custard. When cold, stir in the gelatine (dissolved in 3 dessertspoons very hot water), the rice and the whipped double cream. Transfer the mixture to a pudding basin rinsed out with cold water and put for several hours in the refrigerator. The rice can be frozen in the freezing compartment, though I prefer it simply set but icy cold. Turn out on to a serving dish and surround the base with an orange compôte, or pour over strawberries or raspberries crushed with sugar. Or you can surround it with fresh peaches, skinned and halved and very cold.

VANILLA CREAM

VANILLICREME

5½ dl (1 pint) single cream
3 eggs, separated

120 g (4 oz) vanilla sugar

Beat the yolks with the sugar and cream over steam until thick. When cold, fold in the stiffly beaten whites. Serve very cold.

For COFFEE CREAM, first heat the single cream and dissolve some instant coffee in it before beating with the other ingredients.

And for CHOCOLATE CREAM I, substitute cocoa or melted chocolate for the coffee.

APPLE CREAM

APFELCREME

480 g (1 lb) apples
2 tablespoons strawberry or
*   raspberry jam*

120 g (4 oz) blanched almonds
5½ dl (1 pint) milk
3 eggs, separated

120 g (4 oz) sugar   1 dl (4 oz) double cream

Peel and core the apples and poach in very little water until they are soft but still retain their shape. Transfer the apples carefully to a serving dish, fill the centres with jam and let them get cold while you beat the milk, sugar and yolks over steam to a thick custard. When the custard is cold, fold in the whipped cream and stiffly beaten whites of egg. Pour the custard over the apples and sprinkle with the chopped almonds. Serve very cold.

APRICOT CREAM   KALTGERÜHRTE MARILLEN

480 g (1 lb) ripe apricots   2 egg yolks
240 g (8 oz) caster sugar   5½ dl (1 pint) double cream

Pulp the peeled and stoned apricots with the sugar, stir in the egg yolks and fold in the whipped double cream. Keep in the refrigerator for at least 1 hour before serving. If the apricots are not sufficiently ripe and soft for pulping, boil the stoned fruit in the minimum of water, discard peels and when the fruit is cold proceed as above.

CHOCOLATE CREAM II   SCHOKOLADECREME II

120 g (4 oz) plain chocolate   90 g (3 oz) caster sugar
1½ dl (¼ pint) milk   about 2½ dl (½ pint) whipped
3 eggs, separated   cream

Dissolve the chocolate by breaking it into pieces and bringing to the boil with the milk. Beat the egg yolks lightly with the sugar and, stirring very vigorously, pour the hot milk and chocolate over. Beat the chocolate cream mixture over steam until thick. When the chocolate custard is completely cold, fold in the whipped cream followed by the stiffly beaten whites of egg. Decorate with whipped cream and serve very cold. This cream is very rich.

WHIPPED COFFEE CREAM   KAFFEE SCHLAGOBERS

Make a strong coffee essence from a heaped dessertspoon instant coffee and a heaped teaspoon sugar dissolved in the minimum of very hot water. Whip with about 2½ dl (½ pint) double cream until thick and fluffy. Chill in the refrigerator before serving in individual glasses. Decorate with two halves of a sponge finger in each.

ORANGE CREAM I   ORANGENCREME I

Beat 2 eggs with 120 g (4 oz) sugar and the juice of 2 oranges over steam until thick. Serve very cold.

ORANGE CREAM II   ORANGENCREME II

4 eggs, separated   *3 oranges*
240 g (8 oz) granulated sugar   *2½ dl (½ pint) double cream*
2 dessertspoons rum, optional

Beat the sugar with the yolks until frothy and stir in the rum, if any. Peel the oranges, cut into cubes, and add them to the sugar and eggs. Fold in the whipped cream, followed by the stiffly beaten whites of egg. Keep in the refrigerator for at least 1 hour before serving.

ORANGE CREAM CUPS   ORANGENSCHALERLN

Allow half an orange per person. Cut the oranges in half horizontally. Scoop out the flesh taking care not to pierce the skin. Discard the pips and as much of the pith as possible. Put the flesh through a sieve or in an electric blender. Boil half the orange pulp's weight in sugar with an equal quantity of water until very thick. A drop stretched between thumb and middle finger should form a thread. Stir the syrup into the orange pulp and let it get cold before filling the orange-skin cups. Serve very cold with a spoonful of whipped cream on top of each cup.

PINEAPPLE CREAM   ANANASCREME

5½ dl (1 pint) double cream   *1 small pineapple or a small tin
                                   of pineapple chunks*

Peel the pineapple, slice and then cut into chunks. Fold into the stiffly whipped double cream. If tinned pineapple is used, fold in the chunks and as much of the syrup as the consistency of the cream will allow. Serve very cold.

STRAWBERRY CREAM   KALTGERÜHRTE ERDBEEREN

720 g (1½ lb) fresh strawberries
180 g (6 oz) caster sugar
2½ dl (½ pint) double cream

60 g (2 oz) blanched almonds, cut lengthways

Damaged strawberries can be used for the cream as long as you keep about 120 g (4 oz) perfect ones for decoration. Crush the strawberries with the sugar into a purée, and fold in the whipped cream. Keep for 1 hour in the refrigerator before transferring to a serving dish. Scatter the almonds over. Decorate with the reserved berries.

Raspberries may be used in exactly the same way for RASPBERRY CREAM.

To make STRAWBERRY ICE CREAM, RASPBERRY ICE CREAM and APRICOT ICE CREAM freeze these fruit creams. Stir before serving to dissolve any ice crystals. Transfer to a serving dish and return to the refrigerator until ready to serve.

SPONGE FINGER CREAM   BISKOTTENCREME

Make a thick Vanilla, Chocolate or Coffee Cream (pp. 147–8). Before folding in the stiffly beaten whites of egg, fold in 2½ dl (½ pint) whipped cream. Allow 3–4 sponge fingers (see separate recipe, p. 168) per person. Spread them thinly with apricot jam and arrange in a deep serving dish.

Cover with the particular cream of your choice, and sprinkle with chopped blanched almonds. Serve very cold. For Coffee Cream, let the fingers soak up some sherry (as cheap as you wish).

Desserts

SPONGE FINGER ALMOND CREAM

BISKOTTEN MANDELCREME

3–4 sponge fingers per person
  (see Biscuit section)
about 1 dl (4 oz) milk
150 g (5 oz) butter
4 egg yolks

150 g (5 oz) vanilla sugar
150 g (5 oz) grated blanched
  almonds
about 2½ dl (½ pint) double cream

Arrange the sponge fingers in a deep serving dish leaving a hollow space in the centre. Reserve a few sponge fingers for the top. Moisten the sponge fingers with milk, or sherry. Cream the butter and sugar until fluffy, beat in the yolks, stir in the almonds and fold in the whipped cream, reserving some of the whipped cream for decorating the top. Fill the free centre space with the almond cream, cover with the remaining sponge fingers. Decorate these with the remaining whipped cream. Serve very cold.

WINE CUSTARD

CHAUDEAU

2½ dl (½ pint) white wine
4 egg yolks

120 g (4 oz) caster sugar

Beat the yolks with the sugar until frothy. Stir in the wine and beat over steam until thick. If served hot, the custard can be kept over *warm* water for some minutes, before being served in warmed glasses. If served cold, stir until the custard is cold. Serve with sponge fingers.

ICE CREAM

GEFRORENES

VANILLA: fold 2½ dl (½ pint) whipped double cream into a Vanilla Cream. Freeze in the refrigerator. Half an hour before serving stir the ice cream to dissolve any crystals. Return to the freezing compartment until ready to serve, but don't let the crystals re-form.

This method also applies to CHOCOLATE and COFFEE ICE CREAMS.

Desserts

LEMON ICE CREAM GEFRORENE ZITRONEN CREME

about 2¼ dl (½ pint) single cream *about 2½ dl (½ pint) double cream*
3 eggs, separated *juice of 1 or 2 lemons*
120 g (4 oz) caster sugar

Beat the yolks of egg, sugar and single cream over steam until very thick. Let the custard get completely cold before stirring in the juice of one or two lemons, the whipped double cream and folding in the stiffly beaten whites of egg. Freeze as for Ice Cream.

For ORANGE ICE CREAM, substitute orange juice.

REDCURRANT ICE CREAM RIBISEL OBERS EIS

Pass 480 g (1 lb) stripped redcurrants through a sieve. Weigh the purée in a previously weighed bowl in order to stir an equal weight of caster sugar into the purée. Fold in 2½ dl (½ pint) whipped double cream. Freeze. Stir before serving to dissolve any ice crystals.

APRICOT WATER ICE MARILLEN WASSEREIS

480 g (1 lb) ripe apricots *4 dl (16 oz) water*
240 g (8 oz) lump sugar *juice of 2 lemons*

Put the stoned and pulped apricots through a sieve or in an electric liquidizer. Boil the sugar with an equal amount of water to the 'thread' stage and stir the thick syrup into the fruit purée. Add the lemon juice and the remaining water. Freeze. Before serving give the sherbet a quick stir to dissolve ice crystals. Return to the refrigerator until ready to serve.

STRAWBERRY WATER ICE, RASPBERRY WATER ICE and REDCURRANT WATER ICE are made the same way.

LEMON WATER ICE ZITRONEN WASSEREIS

Juice and peel of 5 large lemons *240 g (8 oz) lump sugar*
4 dl (16 oz) water

Boil 2 dl (8 oz) water with the sugar to the 'thread' stage. Remove from the heat. Stir in the lemon juice and the remaining water. Add the lemon peel and stand in a cool place for ½ hour. Strain through a sieve. Freeze the mixture. When the sherbet starts freezing round the edges give it a good stir and return to the refrigerator until just before serving.

ORANGE WATER ICE (ORANGEN WASSEREIS) is made the same way.

Sweet Sauces and Cake Fillings

VANILLA SAUCE   KANARIMILCH

  5½ dl (1 pint) milk   *60 g (2 oz) vanilla sugar*
  2 egg yolks or 1 egg

Beat all ingredients over steam until thick and frothy. Serve hot or cold with steamed and baked puddings.

CARAMEL SAUCE   KARAMELSOSS

Follow the recipe for Vanilla Sauce (above). Make a caramel from 60 g (2 oz) lump sugar and an equal quantity of water, and stir into the thick hot vanilla sauce.

CHOCOLATE SAUCE I   SCHOKOLADESOSS I

  120 g (4 oz) good plain cooking   *60 g (2 oz) sugar (preferably*
    chocolate   *lump sugar)*
                                ½ dl (2 oz) water

Melt the chocolate over steam or, with a drop of water added, in the oven. Boil the sugar with the water until it forms a thread if a drop is spread between two fingers. Stir the syrup into the melted chocolate. Stir until smooth. If the sauce is too thick stir in hot water, drop by drop, until it has the right consistency. Serve hot.

CHOCOLATE SAUCE II SCHOKOLADESOSS II

Follow the recipe for Chocolate Sauce I (p. 153) but do not add any additional water. Allow the sauce to cool down before stirring in 1 dl (4 oz) whipped cream. Serve cold.

COCOA SAUCE KAKAOSOSS

120 g (4 oz) lump sugar *120 g (4 oz) cocoa*
1 dl (4 oz) water *30 g (1 oz) butter*

Boil water and lump sugar until the sugar forms a thread if a drop is spread between two fingers. Stir the cocoa into the syrup. Beat until smooth. If the sauce is too thick stir in hot water, drop by drop, until the desired consistency is reached. Stir in the butter. Serve hot with desserts.

COFFEE SAUCE KAFFEESOSS

Follow the recipe for Vanilla Sauce (p. 153) and stir into the hot milk enough instant coffee to give a good flavour.

HAZELNUT SAUCE HASELNUSS SOSS

Follow the recipe for Vanilla Sauce (p. 153), but using plain granulated sugar. When the sauce is cold fold in 1 dl (4 oz) whipped double cream together with 60 g (2 oz) roasted grated hazelnuts. To make the sauce less expensive use milk instead of single cream.

VANILLA CAKE FILLING VANILLI TORTENFÜLLE

1 dl (4 oz) single cream *30 g (1 oz) cornflour*
120 g (4 oz) vanilla sugar *120 g (4 oz) unsalted butter or*
2 egg yolks *good quality margarine*

Beat the yolks with a little of the single cream. Stir into the cornflour, and stir until smooth before adding the remainder of the single cream and the sugar. Beat over steam until very thick. Let the custard get cold before stirring it drop by drop into the creamed butter.

CHOCOLATE CAKE FILLING SCHOKOLADE TORTENFÜLLE

*120 g (4 oz) good plain cooking
    chocolate
120 g (4 oz) butter*

*2 egg yolks
60 g (2 oz) icing sugar*

Melt the chocolate over steam or, with a drop of water, in the oven, and stir it into the butter, already creamed with the egg yolks and sugar. Use cold as a filling for cakes and other desserts.

COFFEE CAKE FILLING KAFFEE TORTENFÜLLE

Stir into the ingredients for Vanilla Cake Filling (p. 154) instant coffee dissolved in the hot custard.

HAZELNUT CAKE FILLING HASELNUSS TORTENFÜLLE

Into Vanilla Cake Filling (p. 154) stir 60 g (2 oz) roasted grated hazelnuts.

Icing

Here are a few recipes for Viennese icing made with boiled sugar. I always use them for special occasions, but I must add that I do use icing sugar quite often in icing as well as in cake fillings. However, I never use artificial flavourings of any kind. I cannot think of an instance where the natural product does not give a much better result. I do use unflavoured colourings where the desired colour cannot be produced otherwise.

WHITE SUGAR ICING WEISSE GLASUR

*240 g (8 oz) lump sugar
2 dl (8 oz) water*

240 g (8 oz) caster sugar

Boil the lump sugar in the water to the bubble stage (see my General Notes, p. 177). Stir the syrup gradually into the caster sugar until the icing coats a wooden spoon and can be drawn to a point.

LEMON or ORANGE or COFFEE ICING
ZITRONEN, ORANGEN, KAFFEE GLASUR

Stir enough orange juice, or lemon juice, or very strong coffee essence made from instant coffee and the minimum of hot water, into a White Sugar Icing (p. 155) to give flavour and colouring. Stir until the icing regains the right consistency.

CHOCOLATE ICING
SCHOKOLADE GLASUR

195 g (6¼ oz) lump sugar   *180 g (6 oz) plain chocolate*
1½ dl (6¼ oz) water   *30 g (1 oz) unsalted butter*

Boil sugar and water to the bubble stage (see my General Notes, p. 177). Melt the chocolate over steam. Stir in the butter and stir until smooth. Gradually stir in the syrup until the icing has the right consistency—that is, it will coat a wooden spoon and can be drawn to a point.

Sweet Confections

The following recipes—unlike many Viennese bonbons—are straightforward enough to make at home. These are the ones I have often made myself and can thoroughly recommend.

CANDIED ORANGE PEEL
ARANCINI

Cut orange peel into thin strips. Soak in cold water for 5 days. Change the water several times. On the sixth day drain the soaked peel and weigh. Prepare a solution of two-thirds of the weight of the soaked drained peel in sugar, and three-quarters of the weight in water. Bring the peel to the boil in the solution and simmer until all the liquid has been absorbed. While still hot dredge the peel in granulated sugar and, without overlapping, lay out to dry.

CHESTNUT POTATOES

KASTANIEN KARTOFFEL

240 g (8 oz) chestnuts in their shells or
180 g (6 oz) dried chestnuts
120 g (4 oz) icing sugar

120 g (4 oz) melted plain chocolate
45 g (1½ oz) ground almonds
30 g (1 oz) grated plain chocolate

Make a chestnut purée and stir in the sugar, almonds and melted chocolate. Work into a firm dough. Mould portions of the dough into the shape of potatoes. Dredge in the 30 g (1 oz) grated chocolate. Serve in little paper cups.

CHESTNUT PURÉE BONBONS

GLACIERTE KASTANIEN

240 g (8 oz) chestnuts in their shells or
180 g (6 oz) dried chestnuts

360 g (12 oz) lump sugar
equal amount of water
little wooden sticks

Make a chestnut purée (see separate recipe, p. 117). Boil 120 g (4 oz) lump sugar with an equal amount of water until the syrup coats a wooden spoon. Stir the syrup into the purée and work into a smooth paste. Mould small portions into the shape of chestnuts. Boil 250 g (8 oz) lump sugar with an equal amount of water until it reaches the glazing stage, then spear the 'chestnuts' on the wooden sticks and dip them into the syrup. Dry by sticking the wooden spears into a suitable surface, or laying them—on the chestnuts' least perfect side—on a buttered tin. Let the glazed chestnuts dry in a cool place. Detach from the sticks when fully dry and place in little paper cases or wrap in tinsel paper.

CHESTNUT CHOCOLATE PYRAMIDS

SCHOKOLADE MARONEN

Make a chestnut purée and stir in thick sugar syrup as in the previous recipe. Mould into triangular pyramids thick enough at the base to stand up and tapering off into a point at the top. Cover with chocolate icing. When the icing has set transfer the pyramids to little paper cases.

CHOCOLATES

240 g (8 oz) good quality plain chocolate	*2 egg yolks*
	½ dl (2 oz) double cream
120 g (4 oz) unsalted butter	*cocoa and grated chocolate*

Melt the chocolate in the oven and stir with the unsalted butter until smooth. Stir in the yolks of egg, again stir until smooth and finally stir in the double cream. Transfer the mixture to the refrigerator, and when it is firm enough to handle roll into little balls and dredge in a mixture of cocoa and coarsely grated chocolate. Serve in little paper cups or wrap in silver foil. These sweets should be kept in a cool place and eaten within three days, though they will keep up to a week in the refrigerator.

MARZIPAN

Work 210 g (7 oz) ground almonds with 210 g (7 oz) granulated sugar and 2 whites of egg into a firm paste.

Use other ground nuts instead of almonds for NUT MARZIPAN (NUSS MARZIPAN).

MARZIPAN CHERRIES

Roll out marzipan about 5 mm (¼ in) thick, cut into 5 cm (2 in) squares, and place several glacé cherries in the centre of each square. Fold the marzipan to cover the cherries and roll into balls. Serve in little paper cups or cover with squares of baking film twisted at the ends.

Desserts

MARZIPAN CHOCOLATE BALLS   MARZIPAN KUGERLN

Roll small portions of marzipan into balls, spear the balls on skewers and dip into chocolate icing. Stick the skewers into a suitable surface, or stand them up without touching one another in a jam jar until the icing is hard. Wrap the balls individually in transparent sweet paper or put each in a little paper cup.

MARZIPAN DATES   MARZIPANDATTELN

Remove the stones from dessert dates, and put in a filling of marzipan instead. Re-seal the dates. Serve in little paper cups.

MARZIPAN POTATOES   MARZIPANKARTOFFEL

Mould portions of marzipan into the shape of potatoes. Dredge in a mixture of cocoa and granulated sugar. Serve in little paper cups.

Biscuits and Small Pastries

All the biscuits and small pastries in this section will keep in tins. Although the sweet ones can be served with tea or coffee or to accompany creams or ice creams, they are good enough to be served as a dessert in their own right.

Sweet Biscuits

ALMOND BISCUITS   MANDELPLÄTZCHEN

135 g (4½ oz) sugar
75 g (2½ oz) margarine
135 g (4½ oz) ground almonds,
    not too fine
75 g (2½ oz) plain flour

grated rind of 1 lemon
2 egg yolks
30 g (1 oz) halved blanched
    almonds

Rub the margarine and flour together and work into a dough with the ground almonds, lemon rind, sugar and yolks. Roll out about 5 mm (¼ in) thick, cut into shapes with a pastry cutter, brush over the top with white of egg or cold water, place a blanched almond, split in half, in the centre of each biscuit, and bake in a moderate oven on an ungreased baking sheet for about 20 minutes, until the biscuits are firm to the touch and lightly browned.

The pastry can also be used for GINGERBREAD MEN if you add ginger and spices.

ALMOND CARDS   MANDELKARTEN

210 g (7 oz) plain flour   *grated rind of one lemon*
150 g (5 oz) margarine   *1 teaspoon cocoa*
90 g (3 oz) caster sugar   *45 g (1½ oz) halved blanched*
1 egg   *almonds*

Work flour, margarine, sugar, egg, cocoa and grated rind into a dough. Knead thoroughly and rest in a cool place for a little while. Roll out about 5 mm (¼ in) thick. Cut into rectangles the size of playing cards. Brush over with water or egg, place a halved almond in each corner and in the centre of the rectangles. Bake on an ungreased baking sheet in a moderate oven for about 30 minutes, until the pastry is firm and very lightly browned. Remove from the oven and allow to cool on the baking sheet before carefully removing the cards with a cake slice to a wooden surface.

For CINNAMON CARDS, omit the cocoa and add a heaped teaspoon cinnamon and ½ teaspoon mixed spice.

ALMOND STARS   MÜRBE MANDELBÄCKEREI

180 g (6 oz) plain flour   *grated rind of ½ lemon*
75 g (2½ oz) sugar   *60 g (2 oz) chopped blanched*
105 g (3½ oz) butter or margarine   *almonds*
1 egg, separated

Work flour, sugar, butter, lemon rind and egg yolk into a dough. Roll out thinly and cut into stars or lozenges with a pastry cutter. Brush with egg white, sprinkle with the chopped almonds, and bake in a moderate oven on an ungreased baking sheet for about 20 minutes, until the biscuits are firm to the touch and light brown in colour.

BRAZILIANS   BRASILIANER

150 g (5 oz) margarine   *90 g (3 oz) skinned grated almonds*
150 g (5 oz) plain flour   *grated rind of ½ lemon*
90 g (3 oz) sugar   *coffee icing*

Work margarine, flour, sugar, ground almonds and lemon rind into a paste. Knead. Roll out about 3 mm (⅛ in) thick and cut into rounds with a pastry cutter. Bake on an ungreased baking sheet in a moderate oven for about 15 minutes until the biscuits are firm to the touch and lightly browned. Let the biscuits get cold before icing with coffee icing.

CHOCOLATE BUTTONS   KNÖPFE

135 g (4¼ oz) ground almonds   *1 egg, separated*
135 g (4¼ oz) granulated sugar   *15 g (½ oz) sugar*
135 g (4¼ oz) dark grated
chocolate

Work almonds, sugar, chocolate and white of egg into a firm paste. Roll lightly into balls of about 2½ cm (1 in) diameter, between the palms of your hands. Make an indentation in the tops and fill this with yolk of egg beaten with 15 g (½ oz) sugar. Bake on rice paper in a slow oven until dry. This will take about 1 hour.

ENGLANDERS   ENGLÄNDER

I don't know how these almond meringue biscuits acquired their name. I have never met them outside Vienna, far less in England.

4 whites of egg   *150 g (5 oz) blanched almonds,*
150 g (5 oz) sugar   *cut lengthways into spikes*

Beat the whites of egg very stiffly. Gradually fold in the sugar and almonds and beat over steam until very thick. Scoop out dessert-spoonfuls of the mixture and form little heaps on rice paper on a greased and floured baking sheet. Bake in a slow to moderate oven for about 1 hour, until the biscuits are firm and lightly browned.

HAZELNUT SLICES   HASELNUSS STREIFEN

150 g (5 oz) shelled hazelnuts,   *210 g (7 oz) sugar*
roasted, skinned and grated   *15 g (½ oz) flour*
3 whites of egg

Fold the sugar, flour and grated hazelnuts into the very stiffly beaten whites of egg. Spread on rice paper on a greased and floured baking sheet and bake in a slow to moderate oven until set. When the mixture is half-cooked remove the baking sheet from the oven and quickly cut the mixture into slices with a sharp knife. Return to the oven and complete the baking.

HONEY CAKES   LEBKUCHEN

240 g (8 oz) plain flour, wholemeal if possible
120 g (4 oz) sugar
2 eggs
2 heaped tablespoons honey

cinnamon, ginger and mixed spice to taste
30 g (1 oz) blanched almonds, whole

Work flour, sugar, egg, warmed honey and spices into a paste. Knead. Roll out on a floured board about 5 mm (¼ in) thick. Cut into small rectangles or cut with a pastry cutter into any desired shape. Brush over with lightly beaten egg, place an almond in the centre of each cake, transfer to a greased and floured baking sheet and bake in a hot oven for 20–30 minutes, until the top is firm to the touch and the cakes are nicely browned. Remove from the baking tin to a wooden surface. These honey cakes keep very well.

You can use the pastry for GINGERBREAD MEN and ice and decorate them when cold.

HUSSARS' MOUNTS   HUSARENKRAPFERLN

180 g (6 oz) plain flour
120 g (4 oz) margarine
60 g (2 oz) sugar
grated rind of ½ lemon
1 egg, separated

60 g (2 oz) chopped blanched almonds
strawberry, raspberry or red plum jam

Work flour, margarine, sugar, lemon rind and egg yolk into a dough. Knead. Roll the pastry between the palms of your hands into balls of not more than 2½ cm (1 in) diameter. Make an indentation in the top of each ball with the end of a wooden spoon or with your thumb. Brush the balls with white of egg and dredge them with chopped almonds and sugar. Bake on an ungreased baking sheet in a moderate oven for about 20 minutes, until firm and lightly browned. Remove them to a wooden surface and fill the indentation with a little red jam. This represents the hussar.

BLACK KISSES   SCHOKOLADEBUSSERLN

90 g (3 oz) margarine   *90 g (3 oz) ground almonds*
90 g (3 oz) grated plain   *90 g (3 oz) sugar*
   chocolate

Work all ingredients into a paste. Roll into balls of about 2½ cm (1 in) diameter, between the palms of your hands. Bake in a slow oven on a greased and floured baking sheet for about 1 hour until they are firm to the touch. Turn out and, while still hot, dredge in sugar. Alternatively, let the balls get cold and put a blob of chocolate icing on each.

DATE KISSES   DATELBUSSERLN

3 whites of egg   *210 g (7 oz) cooking dates,*
210 g (7 oz) sugar   *sliced into thin, short pieces*
210 g (7 oz) blanched almonds,
   cut lengthwise into spikes

Beat half the amount of sugar into the very stiffly beaten whites of egg. Stir in the remainder of the sugar with the dates and almonds. Place dessertspoonfuls of the mixture in little heaps on rice paper on a greased and floured baking sheet, and bake in a slow oven until hardened.

You can also spread the mixture out on rice paper on a greased and floured baking sheet, and, when it is half-cooked, cut into long strips, 1 cm (½ in) wide, with a sharp knife. Return to the oven, and when it is fully cooked cut again into 2½ cm (1 in) sticks. Leave to get cold on a wooden board.

HONEY KISSES

60 g (2 oz) honey
120 g (4 oz) sugar
2 eggs
chopped mixed peel

juice of half a lemon
cinnamon and mixed spice
240 g (8 oz) plain flour
ground hazelnuts

Warm the honey and stir into a paste with the sugar, eggs, finely chopped mixed peel, juice of half a lemon, cinnamon and mixed spice to taste, and the flour. Roll between the palms of your hands into balls of about 2½ cm (1 in) diameter, and bake on a greased and floured baking sheet in a moderately hot oven for about 20 minutes, until the cakes are firm to the touch and very lightly browned. Dredge with ground hazelnuts while still hot.

WALNUT CHOCOLATE KISSES

3 whites of egg
150 g (5 oz) sugar
150 g (5 oz) grated walnuts
grated rind of 1 lemon

90 g (3 oz) homemade
  breadcrumbs
150 g (5 oz) grated plain
  chocolate

Work whites of egg, sugar, walnuts, breadcrumbs and lemon rind into a paste. Divide into 2 portions, one containing two-thirds of the paste and a smaller one containing the remaining one-third. Work 90 g (3 oz) of chocolate into the larger portion. Roll between the palms of your hands into little balls of about 2½ cm (1 in) diameter. Dredge in the remaining 60 g (2 oz) grated chocolate. With the thumb make a depression in the centre of each ball and fill with the white mixture. Bake on a greased baking sheet in a moderate oven until firm but not browned.

LINZER TARTLETS

Make pastry as for Linzer Torte (p. 131). Roll out about 5 mm (¼ in) thick, cut into rounds with a pastry cutter and bake on an ungreased baking sheet in a moderate oven for 30 minutes, or until the pastry is firm and very lightly browned. When the rounds are cold, sandwich them together in pairs with raspberry jam and ice with chocolate icing.

CHOCOLATE MACAROONS   SCHWARZE SEELEN

2 whites of egg
150 g (5 oz) sugar
105 g (3½ oz) grated plain
  chocolate

105 g (3½ oz) grated blanched
  almonds

Beat the whites of egg stiffly. Gradually fold in the sugar, chocolate and almonds. Bake on rice paper on a greased and floured baking sheet in a moderate oven until the macaroons are firm but not browned, about 20–30 minutes.

HAZELNUT MACAROONS   HASELNUSSKRAPFERLN

3 whites of egg
150 g (5 oz) sugar

150 g (5 oz) roasted, peeled,
  grated hazelnuts

Beat whites of egg with sugar and hazelnuts until very thick. With a dessertspoon form little heaps of the mixture on rice paper on a greased and floured baking sheet. Bake in a slow to moderate oven for about 1 hour, until set.

WALNUT MACAROONS   WITWENKÜSSE

4 whites of egg
135 g (4½ oz) sugar
135 g (4½ oz) chopped walnuts

60 g (2 oz) finely chopped
  mixed candied peel

Beat whites of egg and sugar over steam until very thick. Stir in the nuts and peel. Scoop out portions of the mixture with a dessertspoon and form little heaps on a greased and floured baking sheet covered with rice paper. Bake in a slow oven until the macaroons are dried. This will take about 1½ hours.

PALM LEAVES PALMENBLÄTTER

Roll out a 480 g (1 lb) packet of puff pastry about 3 mm (⅛ in) thick, into a large oblong. Cover the pastry thickly with granulated sugar. Starting from both long sides roll the pastry into two tight rolls which meet in the centre. With a sharp knife dipped into hot water cut slices about 5 mm (¼ in) thick across the two rolls. Transfer the slices to a dampened baking sheet and bake in a hot oven for 10 to 15 minutes, until crisp and golden brown. When completely cold the palm leaves can be sandwiched together with whipped cream.

CHOCOLATE PRETZELS SCHOKOLADE BREZELN

240 g (8 oz) plain flour   *90 g (3 oz) grated plain chocolate*
150 g (5 oz) margarine

Work flour, margarine and chocolate into a dough. Roll into a sausage about 1 cm (½ in) thick, cut into 7 cm (3 in) lengths and form into pretzels. Bake on an ungreased baking sheet in a moderate oven for about 20 minutes, until the pretzels are firm to the touch. Lift out carefully on to a wooden surface, and when cold put a little Chocolate Icing (p. 156) on each pretzel.

PUFF PASTRY PRETZELS BLÄTTERTEIG BREZELN

Roll out a 240 g (½ lb) packet of puff pastry 3 mm (⅛ in) thick, cut into 2½ cm (1 in) wide strips and twist into pretzels. Brush over lightly with beaten egg, scatter with chopped blanched almonds and sugar, and bake on a dampened baking sheet in a hot oven for 10–15 minutes until the pretzels are golden brown.

SHORTBREAD BISCUITS MÜRBE KEKS

Roll out shortbread pastry (see separate recipe) about 3 mm (⅛ in) thick and cut into rounds or stars with a pastry cutter. Bake on an ungreased baking sheet in a moderate oven for about 15 minutes, until the biscuits are firm to the touch and lightly browned. Sandwich pairs of biscuits together with jam or marmalade.

For SUGAR BISCUITS, brush the cut-out shortbread with egg and sprinkle with demerara sugar.

For ALMOND BISCUITS, brush the cut-out biscuits with white of egg and sprinkle with chopped blanched almonds.

For GINGER BISCUITS, work ginger into the dough to taste. Ice with lemon icing.

SPONGE FINGERS   BISKOTTEN

90 g (3 oz) self-raising flour   *30 g (1 oz) rice flour*
3 eggs   *caster sugar for dredging*
120 g (4 oz) caster sugar

Whisk the eggs and 90 g (3 oz) caster sugar until very thick. Fold in the sifted flour and rice flour. Pipe or spoon on a greased and floured baking sheet in the shape of sponge fingers. Dredge the tops of the fingers with the remaining 30 g (1 oz) caster sugar and bake in a moderately hot oven for up to 20 minutes, until the fingers are light brown in colour. Transfer with the help of a cake slice to a wooden board sprinkled with caster sugar, and dredge the hot sponge fingers all over with caster sugar.

SULTANA BISCUITS   ROSINENSCHEIBEN

60 g (2 oz) margarine   *60 g (2 oz) plain flour*
60 g (2 oz) sugar   *60 g (2 oz) sultanas*
2 eggs

Cream the margarine and sugar until fluffy, beat in the eggs one by one. Gradually fold in the flour. Transfer dessertspoonfuls of the mixture to a greased baking sheet. The biscuits spread during baking, so do not put them too close. Place several sultanas in the centre of each biscuit and bake in a moderately hot oven for about 15 minutes —they should be light brown with a darker edge. Let the biscuits get cold on a wooden board. They keep very well in a tin.

VANILLA CRESCENTS

VANILLIKIPFELN

270 g (9 oz) plain flour
210 g (7 oz) margarine
105 g (3½ oz) ground almonds

105 g (3 ½ oz) caster sugar
30–60 g (1–2 oz) vanilla caster
  sugar

Work flour, margarine, sugar and almonds into a dough. Knead thoroughly and allow to rest in a cold place for about 20 minutes. Roll into one or several sausages of about 1 cm (½ in) diameter, cut into 4 cm (1½ in) lengths and form into crescents. Transfer to an ungreased baking sheet and bake in a moderate oven for about 20 minutes, until firm to the touch. Have ready in a large tin or bowl a thick layer of vanilla sugar to which the hot crescents are transferred. Toss gently back and forth to dredge the crescents all over with the sugar, taking care not to break them. I usually dredge the crescents in the tin in which they will be kept, and when they are completely cold I can simply put the lid on. The vanilla crescents are at their best eaten fresh, but they will keep in a tin for several weeks.

WAFERS

WAFFELN

This is a recipe of Swiss origin. It was brought to my Viennese home by my mother's Swiss governess. I met these crisp and delicious wafers in other Viennese homes, too, and although it is not strictly Viennese I give the recipe here because it is too good to leave out. You will need a wafer iron—I bought mine in a Danish shop in this country.

120 g (4 oz) plain flour
120 g (4 oz) butter
2 egg yolks
150 g (5 oz) caster sugar

grated rind of 1 lemon
about 2½ dl (½ pint) equal
  quantities milk and water, as
  needed

Stir the melted butter, the sugar, yolks and lemon rind together. Fold in the flour and stir in enough of the milk and water mixture to make a smooth—soft but not runny—dough. Let the dough rest at room temperature for several hours. Grease the wafer iron and heat on a gas or coal flame or an electric hotplate. Insert a teaspoon of the mixture in the hot iron, close, and cook for about 2 minutes in the heat of the iron, until the wafer is crisp and light brown in colour. Continue until the dough is used up. Let the wafers get cold at room temperature. They keep very well in an airtight tin.

YEAST BISCUITS   PLÄTZCHEN

240 g (8 oz) plain flour   *60 g (2 oz) margarine*
30 g (1 oz) fresh yeast

Work flour, margarine and yeast—the yeast is not proved—into a dough. Add a little milk, if needed, to make the dough workable. Roll into a sausage of about 4 cm (1½ in) diameter. Cut into 1 cm (½ in) slices, roll lightly into biscuit shape. Bake on a greased and floured baking sheet in a moderately hot oven for 15 minutes, and dredge with sugar while still hot.

Make SAVOURY BISCUITS by dredging the hot biscuits with salt and caraway seeds or salt and poppyseeds.

Savoury Biscuits

CHEESE STRAWS I   KÄSESTANGERLN I

Roll out puff pastry about 5 mm (¼ in) thick, cut into strips 5 cm (2 in) by 1 cm (½ in), brush over with cold water, sprinkle with grated cheese, or with salt and caraway seeds. Bake on a dampened baking sheet in a hot oven for 10–15 minutes, until the pastry is golden brown.

CHEESE STRAWS II   KÄSESTANGERLN II

60 g (2 oz) grated Parmesan or   *105 g (3½ oz) plain flour*
*   Cheddar cheese*   *2–3 tablespoons sour cream*
75 g (2½ oz) margarine   *salt*

Work margarine, flour, most of the cheese and a pinch of salt into a dough. Add enough sour cream to give it the right consistency to be rolled out. Roll out about 5 mm (¼ in) thick and cut into strips about 2½ cm (1 in) by 5 cm (2 in). Brush over with cold water, sprinkle with the remaining grated cheese and bake in a moderately hot oven for about 15 minutes, until the pastry is golden brown.

CURD CHEESE PASTRY STICKS   TOPFENSTANGERLN

Make pastry following the recipe for Curd Cheese Pastry Turnovers (p. 131). Cut the rolled-out pastry into lengths measuring about 1 cm (½ in) by 4 cm (1½ in). Brush them over with water and sprinkle with salt and caraway seed or with grated cheese. Alternatively sprinkle the sticks with sugar and poppyseeds. Bake on a greased baking sheet in a hot oven for 10–15 minutes until lightly browned.

POTATO PASTRY STICKS   ERDÄPFELTEIGSTANGERLN

180 g (6 oz) mashed potatoes   *1 egg yolk*
120 g (4 oz) flour   *salt, caraway seeds*
120 g (4 oz) margarine

Work the potatoes, margarine, egg yolk and a little salt into a dough. Roll out about 5 mm (¼ in) thick, cut into sticks measuring about 5 cm (2 in) by 1 cm (½ in), brush the tops with cold water, sprinkle with salt and caraway seeds and bake on a greased and floured baking sheet in a moderately hot oven until the pastry is golden brown.

SALTED PASTRY STICKS   MÜRBE SALZSTANGERLN

200 g (7 oz) plain flour   *salt*
150 g (5 oz) margarine   *1 egg yolk*
3 tablespoons sour cream   *coarse salt, caraway seeds*

Rub together the flour and margarine, and work into a dough with the sour cream and a little salt. Roll the dough into a sausage of about 1 cm (½ in) diameter, and cut into 10 cm (4 in) lengths. Brush with egg yolk, and sprinkle with the coarse salt and caraway seeds. Bake on an ungreased tin in a moderately hot oven until the pastry is firm to the touch and lightly browned, about 10–15 minutes.

Savoury Spreads and Dips

One can use these spreads in several ways. As sandwich spreads they are at their best on rye bread or on wholemeal bread, or they can be served as a savoury on toast. Try the cheese spreads sandwiched between several layers of Pumpernickel or Vollkornbrot, which are then cut into cubes and served with the cheese course. I often serve Liptauer Cheese (p. 174) and Chives Cheese (p. 174) in a bowl for people to help themselves.

SPRAT BUTTER   SPROTTENBUTTER

240 g (8 oz) smoked sprats   *90 g (3 oz) margarine*

Cut off the heads and bone the fish. Cream the margarine and pass with the roughly chopped sprats through a sieve or put in an electric blender. Add a dash of lemon.

SARDINE BUTTER uses tinned sardines, and ANCHOVY BUTTER salted anchovy fillets, or enough anchovy concentrate to give a strong flavour.

CHEESE TRUFFLES   KÄSETRÜFFELN

120 g (4 oz) each: *Cheddar cheese*
   Gorgonzola cheese   *margarine or butter*
   Danish blue or Roquefort   *1 packet of Pumpernickel or*
     cheese   *similar black rye bread*
   Camembert cheese
   grated Gruyère or

Cream together the margarine and all the cheeses until a pliable mixture is obtained. Roll the cheese mixture between the palms of the hands into balls of about 1 cm ($\frac{1}{2}$ in) diameter, and then roll them in crumbed pumpernickel. The 'truffles' should be well crumbed all over. Keep in the refrigerator for at least 1 hour before serving as a savoury course or with drinks.

CHIVES CHEESE
SCHNITTLAUCH KÄSE

120 g (4 oz) curd cheese
60–120 g (3–4 oz) margarine

30 g (1 oz) finely chopped chives
salt

Cream the margarine with the curd cheese and stir in the chives and a little salt.

LIPTAUER
LIPTAUER KÄSE

120 g (4 oz) curd cheese
60–120 g (3–4 oz) margarine
paprika, salt, French mustard,
  caraway seeds, mixed herbs,

finely chopped onion, all to
  taste
a few drops of beer

Cream the margarine with the curd cheese and stir in the other ingredients. Use enough paprika to give a pink colouring and enough of the other ingredients to give the cheese a strong, pleasant flavour.

SIEVED ROQUEFORT
ROQUEFORT PASSIERT

I must immediately confess that I have substituted Danish or Norwegian blue vein cheese for Roquefort cheese, ever since the latter has become so very expensive.

Use 2 parts cheese to 1 part margarine or butter. Pass the cheese through a sieve and stir into the creamed butter, or put butter and cheese into an electric blender. The mixture looks very attractive lightly forked up in a small serving dish.

General Notes

BAIN-MARIE   Hot or cold water in a pan, in which stands another pan containing the food to be cooked or re-heated.

BAKING BLIND   This is mainly used for baking empty pastry cases and cups. Cover the pastry with greased greaseproof paper on which a small lid or heat-proof saucer is placed. Alternatively cover the pastry with dried haricot beans. This latter method is always used for cup cakes. The beans can be used over and over again. When the pastry is half-cooked, remove the coverings and return the pastry to the oven, filled or unfilled, as the recipe specifies. Complete the baking.

BLANCHING   Dropping food into boiling water or pouring boiling water over. When blanching almonds, let them boil up once before draining into a sieve. The skins will slip off easily.

BREADCRUMBS   Break up dry stale white bread roughly, and dry it in a slow oven on a dampened baking sheet until very brittle. Residue oven heat can be used for this purpose. Make the crumbs in an electric blender, in a hand-operated grinder or with a rolling-pin. Keep the crumbs in an air-tight jar.

CAKE TINS   Cake tins with detachable bottoms have many advantages. Apart from the fact that it is easy to cut the pastry round a base without sides, they make the turning out of the baked cake a very simple operation. Stand the cake tin on a smaller tin and the sides will slip down leaving the cake on the base from which it can be slid off. If the sides do not slide down immediately, exert a little pressure and they will do so. One word of warning: when first putting the cake in the oven put the tin on a baking sheet to catch any drips from the runny mixture.

175

DOUSING   Pouring cold water over cooked food in a colander or holding it for a few moments under the cold tap.

DRIPPING   Render down cooked or uncooked fat, trimmed off or left over from beef, pork, gammon, ham, bacon or poultry. Slice or dice the fat into smallish pieces, put into a pie dish, add a little water and put in a moderately hot oven until the fat has oozed out and the crackling is nicely browned and crisped. Crackling is very good eaten on bread. If it is not being used for this purpose, squeeze out as much of the fat as possible before discarding it. Apart from using it for cooking, dripping is very good salted and eaten on brown bread, particularly goose and duck dripping.

GRAVY FOR ROAST MEAT   Remove the meat from the roasting tin and keep hot while you quickly make the gravy. Pour some very hot water or stock into the pan on a hot-plate, and bring to the boil scraping round with a fork to incorporate all the meat juices at the bottom of the pan. Skim off as much fat as possible. Serve the gravy very hot in a separate dish to the meat.

HAZELNUTS   To roast and peel shelled hazelnuts, put the nuts in an unglazed pan over a low heat. Toss the pan frequently until the skins come off easily when the nuts are rubbed between the palms of the hands. It doesn't matter if little specks of peel stay on the nuts. The nuts can be roasted in a moderate oven, but watch out not to burn them. The hazelnuts can then be ground or grated or used whole, according to the recipe.

MEAT HAMMER   A meat hammer is needed in the preparation of escalopes. Beating and flattening out the meat is essential because of short cooking times. Meat hammers can be bought in most hardware stores. As a substitute, a household hammer with its head tied in a clean cloth can be used.

PASTA   Pasta includes all spaghetti, noodles, macaroni and so on. I always use the eggless varieties—they are cheaper than those containing egg, and I for one cannot taste any difference in the cooked product. Always cook pasta in a large saucepan containing plenty of boiling salted water. Boil steadily until the pasta is soft. Test with a fork or taste a small piece. Drain into a large sieve or a colander and douse under the cold tap. This prevents the cooked pasta from sticking together. The dousing should be done quickly enough not to lose much heat.

POPPYSEEDS   Poppyseeds are used frequently in Viennese cooking. In this country they are less well known and they are usually available only in continental delicatessen shops. A good many of my recipes ask for ground poppyseeds. If a grinder is not available, just cover the seeds with milk and leave them to soak overnight, when they should have softened and have absorbed the milk. Drain off any surplus milk and use as required.

ROUX AND WHITE SAUCE   Use quantities according to the recipe for which the roux or white sauce is being made. Melt the fat over a low heat, soften the onion or other ingredients if any, add seasoning, sprinkle in the flour and continue over the low heat, cooking and stirring for a few moments. Pour on the liquid, bring to the boil while stirring, and stir and boil until any lumps are dissolved. If milk is added this will make a white sauce.

SEMOLINA   I recommend coarse semolina, rather than fine. It has a nice grainy consistency and is less likely to make lumps than the fine variety. It is quite readily available in most good grocers and continental delicatessen shops.

SIEVES   For passing substantial quantities of food through a sieve, I recommend a nylon sieve, on a wooden base about 10 cm (4 in) high, with a fairly large wooden mushroom-shaped tool for pushing the food through. For draining off liquid or for sieving small quantities of food I prefer using a sieve with a handle.

BOILING SUGAR   Use the amount of sugar and water, or fruit juice, indicated in the recipe. Lump sugar thickens faster than any other kind. Use a strong, preferably unglazed, saucepan and dissolve the sugar at low temperature in the liquid. Bring to the boil quickly and continue boiling over high heat. Stir occasionally with a wooden spoon, preferably one which is only used for this purpose. When the sugar masks the spoon, the first stage of thickening has been reached, suitable for jam making. Continue boiling until a drop from the spoon stretched between finger and thumb will form a thread. This is the second stage, for thick sweet sauces. Continue boiling until the thread when lightly blown on will send a little bubble flying away. This is stage three, suitable for icings and for fruit jellies required to set quickly.

VANILLA SUGAR   Have vanilla sugar always ready by keeping caster sugar and a vanilla pod, broken into two or three pieces, in a screw-top jar. Top up the sugar after use and occasionally renew the vanilla pod.

WINE SUBSTITUTE   For about 2½ dl (½ pint) of wine it is possible to substitute 90 g (3 oz) wine vinegar, 30 g (1 oz) sugar, 180 g (6 oz) water.

Index

English

Index

Index

Index

Index

Index

German

Index

Index

Index

Index